MW01603244

most

PUBLISHING

Argentine Nights

Translated by Jana Chisholm

Marek Vácha

First published in English in 2018 by Most,
Bleichistrasse 10, 6300 Zug, Switzerland
info@most-publishing.com
Originally published in Czech as Modlitba
argentinských nocí © Cesta 2011
© Marek Vácha 2011
English language translation © Jana Chisholm 2018
Edited by Derek Blackmore, Isa Hanak and Hamish Cook
Cover design by Joy Paton and Jana Chisholm
Book design by Tomáš Lanča

ISBN 978-3-033-06749-3

Contents

We struggle and know so little about things here on earth. How could we possibly learn about things in heaven?

The Book of Wisdom 9,16

Biology and all its secrets cannot be grasped without feeling like a hungry wolf at least once in our lifetime, or like a ladybird on a leaf, a peacock butterfly in a drop of water or a photosynthesising spruce bathed in light. It is impossible to become a good theologian by studying the views of others only, to write sophisticated reviews, but never feel the human thirst for God. To study the world merely from the outside like an independent and disinterested reporter will never allow us to encompass it. We are walking through life today like we walk through the zoo on Saturdays. This is not the way to meet God; the way of disinterested tourists, who during their walk on the Earth press the shutter from time to time to take a photograph; but rather passionate, longing and hungry for God, longing to find the meaning of things, we exist inside of the world, never outside of it.

Yellow pieces of coal flickered among the smoldering pieces of old logs in the fire and above us, the first stars started to ignite. We were warming ourselves up, sitting around the dying flames in deck chairs holding a glass of red cabernet and we felt really good.

"It is so depressing," said Jana. "I knew you were not doing great, but I had no idea that it was this bad."

"The whole Argentine becomes interesting only from the Andes. I like the part about AIDS. At least once you stand up for Catholics. Saint Therese's dilemma is good, but you should have written it differently," Jana continued. "In general, I gave you either an A or failed you. It is either very good or very bad. Overall, it is very dark and depressing. Kája and I started to read it before bedtime and by chance we chose the story about priesthood. I could not fall asleep!"

"Well, it took you about a minute to fall asleep," Karel corrected his wife.

There was silence for a while, only interrupted by the faint crackling of the fire.

"But you know that you can call anytime and come unannounced," Jana continued seriously.

"Would you have called anybody in that situation, or not?" I asked.

"I don't think so," Jana said after a moment's thought.

"There would have been nothing to say, anyway."

On Tuesday Iva Pospíšilová called from Cesta.

"So Luboš and I have finished reading it. I think the text sits well and can be released as it is.

It is very depressing, but good. The atheists are great, everyone will enjoy reading about how others should behave. According to Luboš, this is like the Tančící Skály for the over 50's."

Then Iva paused for a moment.

"You know that if you needed anything you can call."

"I know," I replied.

On Thursday I met up with Klára. We were preparing the book about a dance under the stars.

"I would definitely keep the chapter about priesthood. It is from real life. And no-one writes about that."

"And it actually happened," I said.

ARGENTINE NIGHTS

—————————————

My friend and I spent a fortnight walking through the Andes. When commitments called him south, I stayed and continued walking alone for over three weeks through the mountains and rainforests exercising my spirit under the canopy.

The most beautiful moments are those spent in absolute solitude. Every evening the decision of where to pitch up is made by one voice. Every evening there is a consensus in what to serve for dinner, but of course it is always the same. The culinary philosophy is simple, totalling half a kilo of food per day. The body takes the other half a kilo from its own reserve. The maths is clear and simple: in ten days a man loses five kilos, in a fortnight seven kilos – here the pilgrim can reminisce with a wry smile the various weight loss trends back home in Europe. Now, back to solitude. If I am taking photos of butterflies for an hour or two, I hinder no one. Should I decide to spend another day or two in Río Pilcomayo, nobody minds. If I leave earlier, nothing stands in my way. Nobody was irritated by the long wait for the stripy *Dryadula phaetusa* butterfly.

No one was bothered. There was no pressure to walk onward. One night in the sleepy woods, a little armadillo *Euphractus sexcinctus* ran under my feet. Here it is called tatú-poju. I would never have thought that an armadillo would be able to navigate its way through tufts of grass and bushes with such incredible speed. Therefore, I made the decision to stay for one more day. There was no need for consultation and no further discussion took place.

The *Heliconius erato phyllis* butterflies, known from the encyclopaedias and textbooks of evolutionary biology, fly live and are much, much more beautiful in real life than on the pages of learning guides. Their flight is a three-dimensional ballet, it appears as if they are about to fall to the ground, yet somehow they always manage to stay up in the air, and then they flap their wings once or twice to propel themselves into the airstream which carries them high up above the branches.

Night falls and a herd of stripy peccary leaves the jungle for the dried out lagoon.

Night bivouac in Gran Chaco, sleeping in the same place for several nights, slowly getting into the rhythm of the jungle, the silence and the madrigal of voices around begin to shape me.

Afternoon in the swamp, observing *carpinchos*, capybaras, and at night watching a couple of toucans playing on the bank opposite me. With the nightfall mosquitos fly in, meaning one has to hermetically close the tent. The jungle comes alive with hundreds of sounds, which leaves me only guessing their origin. Somewhere in the distance monkey chatter echos. Up in the tree next to my camp, I see several frogs and hear a sound, which at my best I am not able to place. Silent rustle of wings, or better still some membranes, as if a bat is repeatedly trying to take off, again and again, being blown into like a sheet of paper. Regardless of the mosquitos, I run out repeatedly, holding my torch. I never see anything. In the morning the tree stands quietly in its place, and even a closer inspection of the bark reveals no crevice or trace, nothing that could help decipher the night's secret. Still, the buzzing and chirping of the night, and then around midnight it is cold and quiet. With nightfall, wearing a headlight, I held a short mass in my tent and all the night cries became the liturgical accompaniment, an unconscious song to consciously articulated prayer.

And later, the Andes. Up in the mountains, one can afford the luxury of sleeping without a tent. There are only *mosquitos* in the lowlands. When I close my eyes, I can see the Argentine sky glowing with stars, the Milky Way, two bright navigation stars Alpha and Beta Centauri and *Cruz del Sur*, the Southern Cross. No luminous haze from the city disturbs the darkness of the mountains. Before going to bed, I always prayed the Rosary. I had never realised how many of its secrets were connected with heaven – Jesus, who ascended into heaven, Mary taken and crowned in heaven by Him. Alone in the Argentine nights, gazing into the dark universe, these rosaries run deeper.

In the Argentine mountains, God is somewhat closer. It is not the domesticated God of our churches or of our confident sermons. It is not the God used by various religious leaders in support of their many ideas, the God whose wishes are made clear by devoted preachers. God, whose advice is interpreted by the established church hierarchy, God of the well situated theologians. The God of Argentine nights is much more mysterious and immense, a more powerful God, who is essential to our survival. Here, alone in the mountains, a pilgrim grasps what it means to live in Him, move in Him, breathe in Him, to be submerged in Him as He shapes us, the same way a violent stream would a trout. Here, a man becomes the image of God, formed by the environment, the *milieu divin*. Fish are shaped by water, birds by air and man is molded by God.

The Argentine sky is black and the Milky Way glows silver, in a way that is impossible to see anywhere in Europe. Into that sky, I was channelling aimlessly my hail marys to God, whose identity is unknown to us. Despite this, we pray to Him, but when we begin to think about what is hiding behind those three letters, we start to fall into a dark vacuum. Philosophy brings us to the edge of the abyss, faith is the step forward into the dark nothing, to God. The mystics all speak about Him as someone different from what we are able to depict, because all of our depictions, the child-like or the most refined theological speculations, were formed somewhere on our little planet, lost in the dark universe above the Andes. God, whom Eckhart calls neither good nor wise, for if something was good, it could be thought of as better and above that, better still. That is not God, for God is the Creator of properties, the Creator of good and wisdom. God who cannot be given any labels. Nothing, God's bottomless wisdom, generosity and knowledge, Unsearchable depths, Impenetrable ways of acting. When Moses asks the Burning Bush, 'Who are you?', God answers, 'That is none of your business, Moses. I am who I am and you will never find my name, for if you learned it, you could rule over me, and manipulate me in the same way as you rule over animals, which I created out of the earth and brought to you, in order to see what names you give them.' The only name that Adam did not learn was God's name, and that is how the cards were dealt.

God, who exists, but somewhat different to man, whose existence is outside space, time and anything tangible. God, who is on a different page, who does not answer prayers, whom we are able to feel but unable to depict, who is not any thing, whom we do call love, but whom we still ask daily not to lead us into temptation. Who is light, but whoever wants to see him, must be blind, and at the same time has to rid God of every "thing".[1]

The gracious God of the Gospels, who is concurrently the Jahwe of Psalm 98, God whose love of man is never-ending, but who at the same time leaves the world under the government and the sun of Satan and who lets his believers plead with Him to deliver them from Evil. God cannot be explained in religious instruction in the same way as one explains times tables or botanics.[2] I feel a bit uneasy when it comes to lectures on the false images of God, for... all our images of God are false.

I taught my college and university students that many times, and often spoke about it during various public lectures. The mountain and its absolute solitude bring the theory to life. Dry, dogmatic theology precepts become more real,

[1] Sokol, Jan, *Mistr Eckhart a středověká mystika.* Vyšehrad, Praha, 2009, p. 227.

[2] Neuwirth, V., *Apokalyptický deník.* Triáda, Praha, 1998, p. 40.

lived through, a man touches the absolute. God, who is Nothing, who is behind all our depictions, definitions, paragraphs and speculations. The mountains and the jungle are where the soul meets God, where there is no longer a need for explanation, submerged in the absolute. Where our reason is put into a great bracket and it is rather the heart that perceives.

Where out of nowhere, new bird and butterfly species emerge from the jungle every day. Where one day, the metaphysical speculations about God took on a completely different meaning, as myself, a lonely pilgrim without a machete, stumbled across a puma as lonely as I. There are moments in the jungle, when a man is able to fully grasp, in one second, what he would never think up years from now in his slippers at home.

The world's great religions teach not to give honour to anything, not even one's homeland, oneself or any ideas.[3] Religion is not a set of views, a set of precepts, a set of sentences about the world. Religion is the air that we breathe, the way we exist in the world and the eyes with which

---

[3] Lash, N., *Holiness, Speech and Silence, Reflection on the Question of God.* Ashgate, England, 2004, p. 10.

we perceive it. The never-ending debates that we Europeans engage in: the disputes between science and faith lack any sense, because the world is one. Not so long ago, it was Europe that came up with the different proofs of God's existence. These were only discussed recently, in the past two centuries. Before that they were meaningless. To the antiquity and the Middle Ages, these questions would seem ludicrous. There are no native peoples known as being atheist, and words like atheism or theism do not exist in any of their languages. It is said that if you meet a native arboreal in New Guinea, with his face painted, calling himself an animist, then he probably studied at Oxford and is on holiday at home. A real animist would never refer to himself in this way. He simply lives within his world. Our faith is similar. The instinctive faith of Argentine mountains, and the faith of intellectual debates that take place in the literary cafes of the pluralist world, over a cup of coffee and a cigarette, are two different things. I am no longer willing to waste time debating the existence or non-existence of God with anybody.

Saint John of the Cross:

I tell you, never draw satisfaction from what you learn about God but rather from what remains disclosed; never waste time loving and delighting in what you learn or taste of God, but rather love and delight in what you cannot learn or experience, for that is what we call: seeking Him in faith.[4]

The paradox of prayer – the more we understand God, the more He becomes unknown.

He who speaks about God through parables does not give a genuine account. But he who speaks about God through nothing, gives his own account.[5]

Solitude is the most beautiful thing. A man returns back to civilisation with the knowledge that he is strong. The strongest of all.

[4] Jan od Kříže, *Duchovní píseň*. Karmelitánské nakladatelství Kostelní Vydří, 2000, p. 38.

[5] Sokol, J., *Mistr Eckhart a středověká mystika*. 3. vyd. Vyšehrad, Praha, 2009, p. 227.

THE SHADOW OF DORIAN GREY

Our great wish is to live without sin, and we try hard to succeed. Still, we fail every time. We are not alone. The priests, monks and the Pope himself are all not very good at it. It seems the institution of the Sacrament of Reconciliation is here to stay a lot longer, not to be deemed as needless yet. For years we have been confessing the same sins. Year by year, limping behind our ideal, like an exhausted marathon runner. No matter what we do, we are still unable to keep up with the man in the lead. It is not possible despite all of the prayers, spiritual exercises and Holy Masses. It is not possible whether we try a little or a great deal. It is not possible in the monastery or in the world.

And worse still, the older I get, the more I drift away from my ideal, and the rucksack I carry is weighing me down with the feeling of grave failure. The Middle School years with my black and white perception of the world, the clear idea of truth and lie, are long gone. The list of sins that I was certain never to commit has alarmingly contracted with age. Why is sinfulness so deeply embedded in each of us, and why is it, that apart from Christ, no-one has ever been able to live a perfect life? Are these really my personal failures, or is there a scheme, something deep inside of me, in the matter from which I have been formed? I do not want to make excuses for my sins, but the fact that we all fail is strange and unexpected. If the ideal is within our reach, then someone should succeed at least once in achieving it. However far and wide, no-one has. Here and there, someone gets close; Padre Pio, Frances, Therese of Lisieux, but I do not know of any others. According to Catechism, it was only Christ and nobody else. In the Old and the New Testament, God makes it very clear. After the flood, Noah makes a sacrifice:

The Lord smelled the pleasing aroma and said in his heart: 'Never again will I curse the ground because of humans, even though every inclination of the human heart is evil from childhood. And never again will I destroy all living creatures, as I have done.'[6]

The close relationship between human sin and the state of the earth, the curse caused by Adam's sin and the story of Noah, in which *as a result of human sin all living creatures on Earth are destroyed* (!) will be discussed further.

In the gospels, Christ touches on this:

'If you, then, though you are evil, know how to give good gifts to your children, how much more will your Father in heaven give good gifts to those who ask him!'[7]

It seems that God has a very realistic picture of man, free of any illusions. Still, why is it like this? Why is every inclination of the human heart evil from childhood? That remains a mystery. Is it

---

[6] Gn 8, 21. (NIV)
[7] Mat 7,11. (NIV)

due to man's freedom, his openness to good and thus to evil, or does the problem lie deeper?

Robert Sacks offers a very stimulating answer in his brilliant commentary on the first chapter of Genesis.[8] In the strict sense, the Creation does not begin until the third verse: *And God said: 'Let there be light,' and there was light.* The Hebrew grammar makes it possible for the expression before and after the conjunction 'and', to be completely identical. Our grammar does not allow it. We would have to translate the verse to either *God said: 'Let there be light,' and let there be light,* or to *God said: 'There was light,' and there was light.* Therefore, what God speaks out corresponds exactly with what really happens. In the following days there is a change. God calls the Creation itself to participate in the work of Creation and things start to happen.

On the third day, God asks the earth to 'grow green' but instead of that, the earth only 'released green'. The exact English translation of this command is: *'let the earth grass grass'* ('grow green'),

---

[8] Sacks, R.D., Commentary on the Book of Genesis, Chapter 1. in Yaffe, M. D., (ed.) *Judaism and Environmental Ethics. Lexington Books*, Lanham, 2001, p. 143-157.

but the earth responds only with *'the earth sent forth grass' ('released green')*. What did God actually want from the earth? We are not sure and it looks as though the earth knows as little as we do, but at the end of the day, God saw that it was good. The earth must have found its own way of responding to God's calling. Still, the earth cannot be sinful, and it appears as though it is trying its hardest to cope with God's demand. Sacks says that perhaps God asks of the earth and the matter the utmost and the earth answers with the utmost possible. Then, in verse 24 *God said: 'Let the land send forth living creatures according to their kinds: the livestock, the creatures that move along the ground, and the wild animals, each according to its kind.' And it was so.* That all happened but immediately it is said in the following verse that God himself had to create all the living creatures: *God made the wild animals according to their kinds, the livestock according to their kinds, and all the creatures that move along the ground according to their kinds. And God saw that it was good.* It seems as though somehow God has to help the earth.

Here, in verse 24, God is using the unexpected term: *send forth*. This is the same word used when the earth answers in verse 12 as it forms vegetation. It seems, Sacks speculates, as though God is officially aware that the world cannot unite in the way he asked of it at the beginning; plan B asks of the earth to do at least what it is capable of. There is a shift from the best to the best possible.[9]

Perhaps in a similar way, the crucified and then resurrected Christ asks Peter in the Greek original if he loves (agape) him and Peter answers using a weaker verb: You know that I love you (fileo). This is repeated for the second time – 'do you love me' (agape) with the answer 'I love you' (fileo). The third time Jesus asks using the weaker verb himself – 'do you love me' (fileo)? and Peter answers: 'You know all things, you know that I love you' (fileo). Some Bible scholars see this purely as stylistic variation, whereas others see Peter, who has already gone through the triple denial, as being timid. With his third question, Jesus comes down to Peter's level and Peter answers every time not with 'I love you' (agape), but 'I love' (fileo). Jesus wants the utmost and Peter answers with the utmost possible.

---

[9] Sacks, R.D., Commentary on the Book of Genesis, Chapter 1. in Yaffe, M. D., (ed.) *Judaism and Environmental Ethics. Lexington Books*, Lanham, 2001, p. 143-157.

A man causes much of his suffering himself. It is my envy, my selfishness and my pride that make the world around me stifling, and when I am unfair to my students, I can hardly blame it on God. Perhaps the first chapter of Genesis wants to indicate that suffering or imperfection have already been somehow encoded into the matter itself. Sacks brings to mind that perhaps man's inability to live according to God's plan is his fault in so much as it is the earth's fault not to be able to grow green or send forth animals – however this is not to be understood in terms of an alibi when it comes to man's free will or guilt. The earth's inability itself could not be the reason to call it sinful at the end of the day. God says it is good. Perhaps, the big question does not lie in the heart of man but rather in the heart of the matter from which he originated. The whole history of creation will become one sad embodiment of this thought. After all, the whole history of creation is a plan B! The whole history of salvation is nothing more than a catastrophic script. Guilt itself is happy *(felix culpa)* but is still guilt. Following their failure, both Adam and Eve are expelled from the garden of Eden, once intended to be permanent and perfect, into the valley of tears. Here Adam's first born Cain, the very Cain who was the first man not to have seen Eden with his own eyes, kills Abel, and triggers off an avalanche of sin that even the great flood waters did not manage to wash away. At some point, after the Tower of Babel, the viewfinder of Genesis leaves humanity as a whole and starts focusing on stories of individual people, in particular Abraham and his descendants, as if it became clear that humanity as such no longer is or ever will be 'righteous'. Much like the flood story, the attempt to eliminate sin in Sodom results in failure. Sin and weakness become permanent companions of man in his return to the Tree of Life. Many Old Testament stories full of blood and sin follow. Later on, it is Christ who must leave Eden and join the man in the valley of tears, in body, within the problematic world, and he resembles us in every way apart from sin. *'He was in the world, and though the world was made through him, the world did not recognise him. He came to that which was his own, but his own did not receive him.'*[10] In our own thoughts about sin, we stumble across the gas grenades

---

[10] John 1,10–11. (NIV)

of the First World War and the gas chambers of the Second. It seems a long time ago, but it has not even been a hundred years. Certainly, it is necessary to work hard in order to improve oneself day by day, but at the same time we ought to bear in mind that we have come from the matter of this earth.

II.

Giving thought to human sin bears great importance. In my opinion, we devote too much time to it – and perhaps we have been unduly worried about it, instead of focusing on following Christ. It is my impression that in our spiritual life we primarily fight against our sins making the gospels into a collection of mandates, commands, prohibitions and permissions, rules and their exceptions and that we as Christians strive first and foremost for sinlessness. During the Holy Confessions, primarily in large cities, one cannot help but notice one thing: the penitents are fully absorbed and completely preoccupied by thinking about themselves to the extent where there is no more space left for their neighbours. And during the Holy Communion they circle each other like aeroplanes would a busy airport.

They are thinking out loud mainly about their own sins, what they did wrong, what they should have done better, what their problem is, they state that they are aware of their sinfulness and are conscious of the fact that it is bad that they sin and that they should not sin, they speculate to what extent their sinfulness has been influenced by their ancestors (family tree became the summer hit). The reality of their own sinfulness and sins themselves zig zag from right to left in their heads, and sometimes because of them, they stop coming to the Holy Communion all together being of the opinion that as sinners they are not worthy of *'communion'*. They are completely oblivious to the fact that this exact prayer, with these very words is being prayed by all present in the church: *Lord, I am not worthy of you to come to me.* Never mind. Saint Teresa of Avila invites her sisters in one of her texts *'do not call out devil, devil, when you can call out God, God!'* by which she tries to say that the primary aim of our life is not to focus on our sin. It does exist and will continue to do so. Perhaps imperfection is somewhat encoded in the very nature of man.

Beware, daughters, of the humility which casts the soul into a deep unrest over the greatness of our sins. The devil finds different ways and torments souls to the extent that they no longer go to the Holy Communion and dare not to pray under the pretext that they are not worthy.[11]

Once again: the only one who lived without sin was Jesus Christ. Other than that, no-one else has ever managed. We are all sinful and at the same time long for holiness. The Catechist views of the church as being both holy – coming from God, and at the same time sinful – formed of people, may apply to every man. The flame of the baptism candle, the flame of holy grace, keeps on burning within us, moving us forward as we struggle with its pace. We wonder how it is possible that the director of *The Passion of the Christ*, a film which has clearly and positively affected many people, could have made such a great mess of his personal life, that even the tolerant Hollywood was disturbed. We wonder how great sinners could have painted beautiful pictures and

---

[11] Sv. Terezie od Ježíše, *Cesta k dokonalosti*. Karmelitánské nakladatelství, Kostelní Vydří, 2002, p. 177.

written captivating poems. The good and the evil, both wheat and weed are somehow sown deeply into our soul. It is only the miniature figures from the advertisements on the Prague underground that could be only good or evil, white or red. We, the real people, are not like that. I am not like that either, being a Catholic priest. When different people look up to me, I wish they could also see the other part of my soul, the picture hidden somewhere in the upper room of my inner being. Oscar Wilde knew very well what he was writing about. How many young men and women told me that they no longer went to church and received sacraments because they were so sinful (usually in connection with the Sixth Commandment), they felt they were not worthy of the Holy Communion and they had stopped praying because they knew that their life was not in order, and at the same time they were aware of their inability to do something about it. Perhaps they already stayed and lived with someone and so on.

I understand that it is good when popes and bishops present the ideal of the pure love and magnanimous self giving etc. during great youth meetings, but I think that apart from the slogans, flag bearing and crowd leading, someone should walk at the back collecting the wounded. Well, could someone from the Catholic readers come up with a solution? In this way our image of the gospel as a list of mandates proves to be very reliable in bringing our spiritual life to a definite halt. Has someone ever said that when I sin, it does not necessarily have to mean the end of everything? How easy and perfectly safe it is to say to a penitent during confession: 'So, when you get rid of your sinfulness, come and I will give you an absolution.' I understand very well how important it is to be consistent, however the consequence of such consistency is a penitent who no longer receives the sacrament of reconciliation nor comes to church. We are very good at pouring water on smouldering wicks and breaking the bent. And I am not thinking about the proud and obstinate now. On the contrary, I am thinking about my ever so humble friends, who are suffering and due to their peculiar honesty, stop praying and living a spiritual life, painfully aware of the fact that they do not come anywhere near the ideals expected of them. And so our understanding of religion immobilises sinners instead of being a motor that would move them further on their way.

The Twelve holy Apostles sinned with such regularity as to be comical. Just like in a film, where every scene makes it obvious that things will not go according to plan. In the New Testament, Peter failed every time it really mattered. Yes, he does say to Christ *if it is you, tell me to come to you on the water,*[12] and then instead of looking at Christ, he sees the wind, becomes afraid and starts drowning. Another time, he comforted Christ in such a way that the founder of Christianity had to let the future Pope have it with the sentence *Get behind me, Satan!*[13], and then comes Peter's triple denial. Still in Gethsemane, he declares that he will follow Christ to his death, and then the maid's first question comes and he crumbles. After the resurrection and the Pentecost, Paul will have to rebuke him – probably rightly so – about the preferential treatment he had given to the Christians of Jewish rather than Gentile descent. On another occasion, the Apostles contest which one is the best among them and later still two of them make a secret pact to beat the rest and sit to Christ's right and left

---

[12] Mat 14,28. (NIV)
[13] Mat 16,23. (NIV)

when the time comes. And so forth. Considering the fact that the Apostles had seen all the miracles and heard all the sermons, Jesus' sin-free pedagogy could hardly be called a success. Yet, the flame he had brought into the world grew strong in the souls of these men, enough to stop all the attempts to extinguish it, spreading all over the Middle East, Europe and after that, the rest of the world.

It is not about how particular we are about what we do but who we are in particular.[14] Following their betrayals, Judas stepped outside and hung himself, and Peter stepped outside and wept bitterly that was the difference. Apart from Christ, there has been no-one completely without sin in this world. And I believe that we are not asked to rid ourselves completely of all our sins and weaknesses. Some Catholic sayings may run deeper than we realise: *'all the devils gone, all the angels too'* or *'if you want to become a martyr, marry a saint'*. I do not believe human nature to be completely corrupt,[15] however, I cannot help

[14] Lewis, C. S., *K jádru křesťanství.* Návrat Domů, Praha, 2008, p. 132.

[15] Viz *Katechismus katolické církve.* Zvon, Praha, 1995, paragraf 405.

but notice that from the Pope to the last believer, we continue to fail when it comes to sinlessness. The material I have been formed from is not pure gold and neither is the life I am living. I wish it was but it is not and will not be. Neither is the earth I have been formed from it sends forth grass in place of grassing grass, and may at least this be the case with me also. *Adam* means a man in Hebrew and *adamá* is earth, man, human, Homo, humus.[16] If I am not able to grass grass, may at least the humus of my body send forth some grass!

It is said that the human soul is like a square house with many rooms and limited access, where it is possible that we are never to reach the garden with a fountain in the middle. At times, following a long period of solitude, we open the door of an unused room and are horrified at the kind of darkness that encompasses us. What kind of matter is it we are from? How did the dark thoughts get inside of me? Which windows, unaware, have I left open, or has the darkness been inside of me right from the beginning?

---

[16] Observed by Zdeněk Neubauer

My ideal about myself and I, the two people chasing each other through the world never to meet; and if that bothers me then I will live my life in continuous trauma. That is not what it is about. What matters is to offer up to God the little of myself, what I have, my five loaves and two fish and out of the little could come so much as to completely exceed my imagination. The sinful Peter becomes the first Pope and dies a martyr death, a tax collector writes a gospel, these sinners give origin to the Hymn to Love, to the book of 1 John, texts which in the course of several centuries turn Europe upside down.

It is therefore perhaps not so much about doing away with our sins but about following Christ, and there is quite a difference between the two.

THE RING IS MINE!

_____

May I be forgiven to compare the unsearchable mystery of Easter with Tolkien. The key Easter event is Gethsemane garden, where Christ prays, *'if it is possible, may this cup be taken from me. Yet not as I will, but as you will.'*[17] A prayer, in which God turns to God, a man without sin to his Creator, a prayer that will not be answered. Christ will go on until the end and die. All the rest that follows Gethsemane is already an avalanche in motion, a logical sequence of steps, going from flogging to crucifixion. The greatest

_____

[17] Matthew 26,39. (NIV)

temptation of Christ takes place in Gethsemane. What happens is not as he wills but as the Father wills. There is still time to get up and leave the scene, leave the actors asleep in the garden and the extras with swords and sticks, to get up quietly and leave for a different country and a different life.

There are no heroes in Tolkien. The great and mighty will never hang the ring round their neck because they know that they are great and strong and that is exactly why the temptation would be too strong for them. Not even the great wizard Gandalf himself, nor the brave Aragorn or the king of the elves. Nobody dares. What use is there in the army manoeuvres and auxiliary battles made grandiose by the filmmakers, when nobody dares to go all the way to the epicentre of evil? The only one that dares is a humble creature without any outlook or ambition, who is perhaps not even able to grasp the full greatness of the task, and even he, at the very end of his test, in his Gethsemane, fails. At the very edge of the cliff, he looks back and shouts to God: 'The ring is mine!' Truly then, the history of good and evil intersects. The evil plays its part and by doing so helps the good. This is the condition of man, for at a certain point during our test we turn to God and say: 'If it is possible, may this cup be taken from me, but as I will. The ring is mine!', we are calling out to heaven. The only one that has passed the test is Christ himself. He, without sin, passes through the test at the cost of His life, because he knows that there is no return from the tunnel and that whoever looks back is not worthy of the heavenly kingdom, but has to die in the fiery abyss with the ring. This is the secret of Christian life: we are winning, even when we lose. God is winning through sinners. We win wars though we lose battles. We struggle to enter heaven using a staircase with the broken steps of the Ten Commandments. Even if every one of us fails repeatedly, against all the odds, good prevails. There is not a single valiant soldier in Christ's army who would never fail. Therefore, the fundamental virtue is not courage, endurance or strength but humility, and so there are not as many great heroes among Christians as there are humble men.

EXPERIENTIAL CHRISTIANITY

The trend is here and has even made its way under the Christmas tree. Apart from the usual presents on Christmas day, we like to give one another experiences: skydiving, exotic holidays, hot air balloon flights and bungee jumping. There is nothing wrong with that. The fact that this is true about our spiritual life is more of a problem. When spiritual activity does not feel as good, we are convinced that something is wrong. During Holy Confession we admit that we do not enjoy prayer, do not feel like going to church, we even have to force ourselves to pray at night and so forth. 'I do not enjoy it, Father,' the penitents complain.

The same happens in the spiritual lives of the young people who are not in regular contact with the traditional Catholic religion. What they desire is a spiritual experience. Young people experiment with LSD, try to meditate in Lotus Position, in the name of Hinduism ignite fiery pujas in the dark, all this in pursuit of new and interesting experiences. When the desired effect does not arrive or they get tired of the novelty of it all, meditation and puja are left behind and they move onto the next thing, the Buddhist Diamond Way, opening of chakras or they turn to master Osho and then to Dr. Steiner, deep ecology or datura tea. And they gather to welcome spring together according to the Ancient Inca ceremony, just like from the children's story about the cat and dog, making a birthday cake using all they could find in the house. The way to adrenalin could be through long journeys into unknown territories but also through the journey inwards into the heart. Intoxicated modern psychonauts give expert talks on conscious cosmic solidarity, while being completely useless in real life. It reminds me of uncle Franz from the book Saturnin: say nothing to me, just give me a ruler and compasses and I will figure it out myself.

Most importantly, no commitments or pain, everything is allowed and nothing compulsory. A quick fix. Just like fast food, we try fast religion. The strongest spiritual enjoyment with the least effort, through chemicals or holding one's breath. Either way, let's go for it.

Similarly, this is reflected in the spiritual life of young people who attend church. When I attend their upbeat services, they sing with a guitar that all is well, all the more happy we follow Christ, the Lord God loves us and we love him, the most beautiful moments are on our knees, by love they know us Christians, alleluia, hosanna, Jesus Christ loves us, we are all one body and you can have love in your heart every hour and every day. Spread your wings and fly. Jesus loves you, Jesus friend.

If the people, young Catholics, feel absolutely nothing during these songs, or even feel a bit embarrassed, logically they confess that the service did not bring them the right enjoyment and being good Catholics, they blame themselves for it.

What now? There are many ways of worship and no official regulations demand the involvement of everyone in all of them. If I find the children's interactive songs about dandelions in yellow hats a bit infantile, it does not necessarily signal a personal burnout but rather the natural process of maturing. It is not required that we do it all.

If I do not feel like going to church, that is not a sin, that is a fact. Similarly, if I have to force myself to make time for an evening prayer, that is not a sin, that is a fact. The Catholic faith is not primarily about an experience but is about a relationship, the decision to have a relationship, no matter what it takes. Sometimes we are under the impression that if we are not able to act naturally and we have to use our will to force ourselves to do certain things, there must be something wrong. We blame ourselves for our inability to live in harmony with our inner being, reciting our empty prayers as we go to sleep questioning if there is any point to it all.

But there is. I am a great fan of mumbled prayers and Holy Masses spent with an absent mind. I have great respect for every prayer spoken with great struggle. I am a big fan of the Rosary, even when late at night it makes one fall asleep. St. John of the Cross from 1582 to 1585:

> *[Beginners] They approach prayer in the same way; they believe that its main purpose is to find pleasure and piety and they strive to achieve this, as they say, with their arms' strength. (...) When an exercise is not to their liking, they suffer and approach the matter with great distaste and aversion, refusing its repetition or abandoning it all together; and doing so, as it has already been said, they resemble children, who are not drawn by nor act upon reason but feelings.[18]*

It may be that what has been said about prayer resembles our students' situation; every evening they study because they believe that it is important. Once in a while, a student could find the textbook interesting enough to stop watching the time only to realise that it is three in the morning. This happens, but not so often. Usually, one has to force oneself to study and surely that does

---

[18] Sv. Jan od Kříže, *Temná noc.* Karmelitánské nakladatelství, Kostelní Vydří 1995, p. 59-60.

not come naturally or in harmony with oneself. Yet, one still does it because it makes sense! To get up every day at the sound of an alarm clock is against our nature. If lovers or engaged couples decide to stay together as long as they are having fun, their relationship cannot survive. If students study hard only when they are having fun, they will learn nothing. If parents bring up their children only when it is pleasant for them, they will bring up no-one. If Christians pray only when it is emotionally satisfying they will not get anywhere.

When asked by the press what a prayer brings to a priest, we priests usually answer that it brings a certain calm, peace, concentration and that in the silent, cool church we find rest from the turmoil of the day. The press like to write this down and print it because it is easy to understand. However, this reduces prayer to only one of the possible meditations for the peace of mind. Some practice yoga, others, in the hope of finding peace, use marijuana or take a pill and others still simply pray. Readers could try prayer too and if it does not work then they could try something else, perhaps Sri Chinmoy meditation, go on an angel communication course or drink herbal tea. What does prayer actually give us? Jeremiah's response coming from the muddy cistern would probably be different to the response given by the participants of a youth meeting. What does Jeremiah get out of his faith, standing waist high in mud? Now and then, every believer utters a sigh when they imagine how much simpler life could have been without faith. Not as complicated, more straightforward and we are right in our observation. Prayer is not so much about enjoyment or peace of mind but about a decision, a relationship.

Theoretical pedagogy competes in its attempts to make learning more interesting, as it tries to maximise the concept of learning through play in order to make school even more enjoyable for children. As a result, a whole new field called 'experiential pedagogy' came into being. Practical pedagogy is all the more sceptical. It considers 'cramming and memorising' as the necessary prerequisite. The fact that Arthropoda is divided into Trilobitomorpha, Crustacea, Chelicerata and Hexapoda is not fun or uplifting, but one has to learn it, has to memorise it, otherwise he or she will be stuck with regards to invertebrate zoology. Failure to grasp this at university level gives me no option but to fail students, to my great embarrassment. I am very fond of memorising poems and the cramming of boring telephone lists. It is only this way that allows our head later to make unexpected connections at the right moment and come up with something new, a new invention. The idea that it is no longer necessary to learn as much because everything could be found on the internet is an illusion supported by the lazy.

This is the reason why Catechism insists on the regular Sunday Mass, everyday prayer and regular partaking in the Holy Sacraments. I consider this routine of daily commitments and their fulfilment essential. Tick, tick, no brainer. Attending church during happy times, when I feel fulfilled and can feel God's presence everywhere, every second of every day, that anybody can manage. I am not making fun of feelings. Emotions are a gift from God and thanks be to God for them. Attending a church on Sunday with its unpleasant early rising, praying in the evening when seventeen completely legitimate reasons make it seem impossible at the time, and furthermore when there is 'nothing in it for me', dedicating my time to God automatically, that is something not just anybody can manage. It is these Catechist obligations that form a frame, an iron construction of order and an armed vehicle which takes us through the desert to better times. Anybody can manage a walk in the garden, it is the trekking through a desert that is not for everyone. In his many discussions with the Pharisees, Jesus never questioned the structure, but he made it clear again and again that a mere structure in itself is not the end of the story. Non-experiential Christianity makes it past the heavenly gate. It is not a coincidence that the most famous work of Catholic mysticism is not called 'Bright Day', but 'Dark Night'.

BLESSED BE YOU,
CREATURE OF WATER

I.

First, some theory. 20th century philosophy focused on language as one of the main issues. According to philosophers, two scenarios can take place when we speak. Our speech could either be an informative act or a performative act. If there is an earthquake in Haiti or a Czech speed skater wins the olympic gold medal and the TV presenter makes an announcement about it, this is an informative act. The earthquake has already taken place and the speed skater has already won, and all of it happened regardless of tonight and our ability to find out about it. It is a fact, and nothing can change it, whether everyone on this planet knows about it or not. In this case, speech is an informative act.

Other times we can say something performatively. Something is said and with the same speech comes a reality that has not existed before, but now it does. A typical example would be a court ruling. At the end of the trial everyone rises and the judge reads the verdict – the defendant is freed and goes home. The bride and groom say 'I do' in the registry office and become legally married. I call out 'hello' to someone and thereby engage in an act of greeting.

We know performative words from fairy-tales. The wizard casts out the appropriate spell and things start happening. It is enough to speak out the correct version of the spell, for the rock to open. When we read in the book of Genesis Isaac's blessing bestowed upon Jacob, we as Europeans can hardly envisage this act. Isaac is already old and his sight is poor, and because he feels the end is near, he wants to bless his first-born son. His first-born son is called Esau. The Bible reveals that his arms and neck are hairy and Isaac loves him very much. Esau is a hunter and Isaac loves game, or at least that is how the book of Genesis puts it. It is decided that Esau will catch something, prepare it and after the meal he will get his father Isaac's blessing. Up until now, all is well. However, the situation is a bit more complicated. Isaac's wife Rebecca has more love for the younger twin brother Jacob. She devises a ruse while Esau is hunting. She persuades Jacob to wrap his arms and neck with fur, and then Rebecca quickly prepares a meal from their goat. Jacob, disguised as Esau, presents the meal to his father as the catch. Isaac is amazed that Esau came back from hunting so soon. He eats, and when it occurs to him that the voice belongs to Jacob, his touch tells him that it is Esau by his side. Furthermore, Jacob is wearing Esau's clothes, and so the smell is also Esau's. And so Isaac blesses Jacob. Then Esau comes back from hunting, prepares the meal and goes to his father Isaac, as agreed, and all is revealed. There was nothing that could be done about Jacob's blessing! We Europeans would say, that after all nothing has changed, everything has probably taken place in a tent somewhere in a semi-desert, and the whole issue has been dealt with between the four of them, involving nobody else! And still a blessing, just like a spell, once it has been cast, it does its job and it is impossible to take it back. Isaac blesses performatively. The blessing, once given, is already aflight like an arrow and does its job. It is not possible to revoke it. This is difficult to understand for us Europeans, because we have learnt that even the registry office can revoke our marital consent, the agreement annulled, the piece of paper torn, the promise questioned and the arranged meeting postponed by our mobile phones to a different time, a different place or cancelled altogether. We say something and then take it back, we pronounce something and then apologise. We passionately declare our love today and take it all back tomorrow, claiming that it was spoken in the heat of passion. The day after tomorrow, we confirm that we are no longer in love, and the following day we correct ourselves saying that we did not mean it after all. The next day we say sorry and profess our love, again and again we declare eternal peace – until the next war. Today words are nothing, words do not become flesh, they are mere oscillate air waves, nothing more. They can be bent to the right, to the left, backwards and forwards, up and down, as it is required at the time. They express the immediate feeling of the speaker, the current impression, nothing more and nothing less. Tomorrow or in five minutes, things will be completely different. No harm done; here a promise, there a promise. That is not the case with Isaac. The word is pronounced and it is not possible to take it back.

The mystery of the word is important in many other places in the Bible. Every time the God of the Old Testament speaks, he speaks performatively! Let there be light the Yahweh commands, and it is so. These are the first words God speaks in the Bible. Let there be an expanse between the waters to separate water from water, says Yahweh – and it is so. The ground appears, the land produces vegetation, waters teem with living creatures, every living and moving thing and every winged bird according to their kind. Every living creature and plant is the word that became flesh. Yahweh speaks and it comes to pass. As the rain falls on the ground and the land produces vegetation, so does the word of God. It flies like an arrow, does its job and never returns without avail. The letter to the Hebrews begins by stating that in the past God spoke to our forefathers through the prophets on many occasions and in various ways, but the last word Yahweh spoke was Jesus. And the word became flesh and dwelt among us. *Vajomer Elohim*, God spoke and the world was created. The world originated through the Word and the Word shines in the darkness and the darkness has not overcome it. Wow.

We teach this to the children in Sunday school together with the holy sacraments. The administration of the sacraments is performative. The priest says: *John, I baptise you in the name of the Father and the Son and the Holy Spirit,* and the child is baptised. *Receive the seal of the gifts of the Holy Spirit.* And John later says: *I, John, give myself to you Mary, and take you as my wife. Take and eat all of you. I grant you the absolution in the name of the Father, and Son and the Holy Spirit. Lazarus come out. Your sins are forgiven. Effatha. Talitha Kum.*

II.

At times my work commitments bring the duty of taking part in graduation ceremonies. The novelty comes in standing on the other side of the barricade, so to speak. One look at the overcome parents and grandparents and it would be hard not to see how much we need rituals.

The Holy Mass, or to be precise, confirmation, is strikingly similar. To begin with, all present put on a black gown, because it would be hard to come to a wedding feast without a wedding gown. We cover our heads with a strange black hat which is not called a biretta, but could be. Then we enter the hall in the typical formation we are used to from churches, the less important first and the most important last. Pedell with the silver sceptre enters first followed by the proud members of accademia with the spectabilis Dean and honorabilis Vice-Rector at the end. The organ above plays the melody of the song *Jezu Kriste, ščedrý kněže*. No need to add that all are standing. Before the podium the procession splits in the middle heading for the seats right and left in the given order, and once the honorabilis is seated, all present sit down, customary to church. The promoter begins the ceremony by calling the spectabilis Dean to give his speech. The Dean calls the students to adhere to the rules of ethics and his speech makes sense. Honorabilis comes next with his contribution, a bit more vague, stating the obvious truths about the increase in knowledge in all scientific fields over the last four hundred years, and without any further elaboration on this important thought, the honorabilis jumps to a different topic and states that our renowned university is proud of our students, and they should also be proud of it – their Alma Mater, and they should never forget this day. This 'word mass' is followed by the initiation ritual. The Spectabilis in his performative act appoints the students as doctors of general medicine and the students respond ceremonially *spondeo ac polliceor* with their hand touching the scepter as they make their oath. The congratulations follow, the parents are moved, the grandparents cry. At the end, the organist plays, again without lyrics, *Gaudeamus igitur* and we all leave. The initiation ceremony, a boy becomes a man, a child becomes a mature Christian, a student becomes a doctor. The Catholics have confirmation, the Jews bar mitzvah and Lakotas after the ceremony of inita leave to meditate in Black Hills. All cultures have it.

I remember, as a boy brought up under the religion of communism, a gathering in the local cinema, where we, the students graduating from the last year of primary school, were dressed in dark jackets with awkwardly tethered ties, the bolshevik rock band playing, as we received, in a bizarre ritual, our first brand new ID cards. On that famous day, there was no school. We were no longer children but men. Before we taunt this caricature of habit, it is worth remembering that rituals both the atheist and the Christian are not a modern invention, but started possibly somewhere on the African plain, when we danced our first initiation dance around the fire and then again and again. We are not rational beings who become emotional from time to time. We are emotional beings who occasionally use reason.

I wish confirmation was the sacrament of initiation once again, connected to a long preparation, long fast, acceptance of a new name with the confirmee taken seriously as an adult and a responsible member of the community. If we refuse responsibility, we remain a culture of youngsters where our politicians and TV series action heroes behave like adolescents; a culture of neoteny with immature axolotls brought up by immature parents and immature teachers. It is only children who can grumble about the iniquity of the world; the adults already know that the world is their responsibility, that it is their world and that their reproach should be directed the most at themselves.

Once I attended a ritual to welcome spring, a barefoot dancer wearing a special tie-dye dress was dancing on the bare ground, pounding the ground with her fists and we, the spectators, were watching and clapping politely at the end, half a theatre, half a prayer to the pagan gods. This took place near a spot where the oldest church in Bohemia used to stand, and a similar ritual could have been played out here a hundred or a thousand years ago, always in spring. During the dance a jet flew over our heads leaving a vapour line in the sky. Yes, the human mind functions well in technology and science, we keep on moving forward through centuries, the deeper parts of our soul are left untouched. We fly jets and deep down below a dancer is writhing on the ground and the onlookers understand it as a little bit of folklore and a little bit of realism. Konstantinus and Methodius have only just been a second ago, a thousand years, and Christianity seems to be nothing more than a fine layer of colour coating, a peeling layer of thin paint on man's soul, with Perun and other nameless deities of the past grinning at us from underneath.

I reviewed a text for a magazine a while ago, along a similar line of thinking. The author, a famous scholar, defined myths in his philosophical article as false fables, and we all know that today, the text read. In the footnotes of my review, I wrote that it could no be so easily said. The meaning of Mythos and Logos is indeed 'word' but each of them signify something different. In his reaction to my review, the professor argued that myths *are false!* after all. It is a lot more complicated. When seated around the campfire with a song '*... from a derelict church, in a box with a piece of soap, I brought back an angel, his wings they broke...*' What are our medical students really doing? Are they lying or not? Well, that is not the point, is it? It is not the job of a myth to provide us with new and previously unknown information. The purpose of a myth is to induce a feeling of solidarity; the task of a myth is to connect with the deeper layers of personality, as opposed to the rather intellectual surface of the soul. The primitive mentality *does not invent* myths, but *experiences* them, writes Jung.[19] Myths somehow emerge within us and we merely express them. Similarly, again and again different catechists come up with the question about the first chapter of Genesis, after all it is written there in black and white that the world was created in six days, and so is the

[19] Jung, C. G., *Archetypy a nevědomí.* Výbor z díla, svazek II. Nakladatelství Tomáše Janečka, Brno, 1998, p. 231.

Bible really right or wrong? Well, yes, it is right, I reply, but on a different level. The author certainly was not a journalist following God with his little notebook writing down each day what was created and how. The truth is, the author was not there and basically could not have been there, at least not until the sixth day. The author clearly was not a university lecturer in astronomy or natural history either and most probably his was not the desire to share with the readers of the Bible his take on quantum mechanics or the genetic drift.

When it comes to the truth, perhaps it is not as complicated. Above every door of the Prague underground, we can see the familiar rectangular map of the three lines running through Prague, where the three individual lines, green, yellow and red, are drawn parallel to each other with only the middle part slightly looped, in order to intersect in three junctions. Every stop on every line is drawn the exact distance from the other. Well, now if we are about the pure and final truth, we would have to say, that there is almost everything wrong with this picture: in reality, in actual Prague itself, there are various turns on the lines, and stops are spaced unevenly. Well, now what? Is the map right or not? Of course the answer is yes, but only in the fact that there are three lines with stops coming in a linear sequence and that at some point these intersect. We always have to pay attention to the author's intention, what truths he wants to communicate to us and what is left open to interpretation. However, we have digressed.

Our fondness of sitting around the fire with a song does not come from our generation itself, we have been doing it for more than a hundred thousand years, our forefathers did it with their forefathers and it is not possible to simply erase the whole thing in the course of one century purely because now we live in a block of flats and drive cars. Not even our fascination with fire and our gazing at the flames come from our compulsory 21st century school attendance, we have learnt this much earlier. One more experience which served me as a window into the evolutionary dusk. The year of my diaconate, a youth disco, three o'clock in the morning. A man and a woman improvising to the sharp rhythm of the music, or perhaps still, a boy and a girl, both in their twenties, both can do it and both are my friends. He is dancing aggressively, she is retreating, but rather orbiting, faking retreat, she is letting herself be pushed, yet looking closer at her I realise, it is in effect she who is in charge of the motion, the music is absorbing everything and the dance floor keeps on shaking in its rhythm. The message is plain, it would be understood by both Australian aborigines or African nomads. No need for any professions, all is said more clearly than anyone could in a flood of words. Neither of my friends invented the dance, I have realised, they were dancing in the way they knew they ought to, and as they had learnt more than a hundred thousand years ago.

The present Pope Benedict XVI. allowed the observation of the Tridentine liturgy, and we no longer understand why. In the second half of the 20th century, the liturgy has undergone significant simplification and rationalisation. There are only two candles burning on the altar, the priest's dress is relatively simple and modern churches are constructed in a way which allows one to gather around the altar and breathe down the priest's neck, watching. With the exception of the sermon, the priest is not able to improvise, but only to read the text prepared in advance, accessible to everyone. All is lit up with bright electric lights, no space for shadows, all is balanced, squared, logical and intelligible. Liturgy has become the reflection of our rational heart.

Similarly, nowadays we have resigned our idea of marriage saying that when we love each other there is no need for a special ceremony, that we are simply together and that is it. Intellectually it stands, but again and again we give ourselves logical and rational justifications for this step. We have definitely no need to shake hands with an old man from the town hall who wears a funny medal around his neck and recites poetry, that is for sure. However, late at night, when we wake up and cannot go back to sleep, it feels like something is missing. The fact is, all of us, the engaged couple and their friends, feel the need for the tribe to get together, for the wampums to be sent out with the *your presence is requested at*, for the special clothes to be put on, for the bride to arrive in her white dress, all dressed up with special jewelry, as always, as it once was, for us to all line up for the wedding march with the bride walking through the middle, for the priest to give his speech, which we are not going to remember, to hear the promise and see the kiss, to partake in the Body and the Blood of the Lord – what has reason got to do with it? To give gifts just like a hundred thousand years ago, to have a feast and then dance and when we all go to sleep at night to know that something old has ended and something new has begun. That the earth has burst, swallowing up the old and giving birth to the new, that we have heard the quiet purring of its inner drums, that all of us veteran husbands and wives held hands during the wedding ceremony feeling the shivers running down our spine.

Perhaps that is why the Pope is referring back to the Trident liturgy, maybe it is not about traditionalism or modernism, disputing theological streaming but about something deeper, a deeper current, that something within our soul, hard to express. In Orthodox and Greek Catholic temples the most important parts of the Holy Mass take place behind the iconostasis, where believers are only allowed to look in. Sometimes Latin in its incomprehensibility is said to have been the iconostasis of the Western church, playing the role of the barrier, dividing the world here from the world there, a language barrier between the secular and sacral world. We do not understand the fairytale incantations either, as they are normally delivered in an incomprehensible language, the ancient language of the dead. However, nowadays we go further and ask ourselves to what extent the different church regulations are binding. In order to obtain the full indulgence, we are expected to go and pray at the cemetery on All Saints Day and a true Catholic should visit the cemetery if possible every day between the second and eighth of November – and we ask why. Can God not hear me praying for the dead when I pray at the school chapel? Is my prayer not the same regardless of it being delivered at the bus stop, on the tram or in my room at home – do I really have to do it at some special location? And are these full indulgences not obtainable, let's say the morning of the ninth of November or perhaps in July? We have no rational answer for it, we shrug our shoulders and without any clarification say that this is simply how it is done.

In the same way we question why we must bury our dead. They do not care anyway. It is becoming a custom especially in Prague and bigger cities to have the state pay for one's cremation and to scatter the ashes on the ash meadow, no need to get together, it is what it is, the dead does not care and we do not need it after all, we loved him and do not need to prove it to ourselves with an expensive funeral. We do not do funerals because they are logically unjustifiable and when we are invited by another family, we do not attend. Jokingly, with a tinge of black humour – the dead are not coming to ours either. The dead do not care, all is dead to the dead.

Yes, the dead do not care, but we do. The dead need no ceremonies, but we do. As usual the evolutionary past has caught up with us, and it does not matter if we call it collective ignorance or genes made by the blood passed onto us through the old ancient four legged Saurs, still gurgling in our veins. To cut the long story short, we need to once again put on the special black suit and the black tie, we need to get together. Once again, as we are already used to, at the crematorium or the church, the organist playing and we rise as the priest makes his entry. We need to hear his speech, no matter how much of it we will not remember. We need to hear and speak out prayers, see the priest sprinkle the coffin with the holy water and walk around the candle in front of the coffin with the censer burning incense. We need to see the burial party lift the coffin up and down three times at the doorframe of the house or the church. In Lechovice or Bozice we need to hear the same old music played by the funeral band in front of the church, accompanying the coffin with the deceased all the way to the cemetery. We need to see the acolyte at the head of the procession with the cross adorned with a black ribbon, which is later on thrown into the consecrated grave. After the ceremony, we need to hear the priest say that *in the name of the grieving family, thank you for your presence and your prayers. And on behalf of the deceased, I ask you, if he has wronged anybody during his life through God's grace may you grant him pardon.* And relieved we add *may the Lord forgive him*, we throw our little shovel of soil on the coffin, give our condolences and then go to the feast, where we eat, reminisce and say our goodbye. Through this ritual we have concluded our relationship with the deceased, we made a full stop and if he ever comes to visit us in our dreams (this usually happens here in Moravia) then always on good terms. They do not need it but we do and it has nothing to do with reason.

On All Saints Day, we need to make our way to the cemetery, to listen to the talk of the tomb stones in a drizzle and pray in the bleak fog for our dead standing around us.

It is not possible for any society to live without its rituals. As a young boy, I used to go to church on purpose and in defiance of my parents wearing clothes I would normally use for the greater outdoors, because I considered it special as opposed to my Sunday best which evoked in me many unpleasant memories. The Sunday Holy Mass in the city almost resembled a fashion show from time to time with women showing off their new outfits. We were very sensitive to that. Village life is different, more sincere and the term 'Sunday best' is still a technical term. Nowadays I no longer laugh at the Sunday best, Sunday lunch or Sunday concert.

III.

On Easter Sunday in Lechovice, I use Paul VI.'s missal from 1968. It is only forty years old! Easter Saturday, the only day without liturgy, crosses covered, the darkness of the primordial chaos. Today the world will be created again! Long after the sunset the fire is lit in front of the church, we light it with the sacred flint or using the wooden spindle and fire board, the Paschal candle is anointed and the prayer brings the first dark and heady whiff of mystery.

Therefore, Heavenly Father, in the joy of this night, receive our evening sacrifice of praise, your Church's solemn offering. Accept this Easter candle, fashioned from the work of bees, a flame divided but undimmed, a pillar of fire that glows to the honour of God. Let it mingle with the light of heaven and continue bravely burning to dispel the darkness of this night. May the morning star, which never sets, find this flame still burning. Christ that morning star, who came back from the dead and shed peaceful light on all, your son, who lives and reigns forever and ever. Amen.[20]

Exsultet is sung in a quiet dark church with only the paschali and the candle of believers burning, a song through which the world is created again, a song through which the order rises from the primordial chaos, a song of the first chapter of the book of Genesis, a song through which a flickering flame comes out of darkness and grows with the lyrics of the hesitant tentative song. Wax the sign of the old and the new.

---

[20] Praeconium paschali Exsultet www.saintmeinrd.edu/media/28508/Exultet.pdf

Here, wax is a symbol of something that appears to have survived the end of the world and even God's death itself, so that through this the risen God could renew his creation and restore the world order. If Paschali is the symbol of continuity and stability of the world (with it the baptismal candles will be lit throughout the year) then its wax form expresses the creational substance, the base of its connection between the end and the beginning, theogony and cosmogony.[21]

I pour out the baptismal water into the four parts of the world, I breathe on it three times forming the twenty-third letter of the Greek alphabet 'sai', I touch it with the sacred oil forming a cross and dip the paschali in it three times, deeper every time. I use ancient prayers. It is not so much the words that are important but their rhythm:

May those who are different in gender or time be reborn through grace as the mother. Cast out, Lord, every unclean spirit, with all evil deceit

[21] Neubauer, Z., *Mystéria křesťanská aneb o kosmogonickém tajemství Velikonoc.* Malvern, Praha, 2009, p. 20–21.

and malice. May no evil spirits exercise their power, no malice encompass us, no darkness creeping in to dishonour and destroy.

Then I, the priest, touch the water with my hand to indicate that it ought to be sanctified and thus predestined for sacred purposes only. Again I am under the impression that from the deep of the earth the sound of drums is echoing, as the same words have been uttered over the past hundred, thousand, million years, since our species started to walk the earth. The animist times are coming, animist times that cannot tell the difference between the divine and substantial, between a person and a thing, between the spiritual and the materialistic:

Therefore be blessed, Creature of water, through God + living, through God + true, through God + holy; through God who spoke at the beginning and separated you from the land; whose Spirit was hovering above you.

Creature of water! Using his hands, the priest parts the water and at the same time spills a bit in the direction of the four parts of the world in order to demonstrate that it it through sacraments that God's grace is to be poured out into the whole world and exhilarate people of all nations, as Christ has commanded.[22] Blessed be you, Creature of water.

The tribe gathers around the shaman and once more the world is created.

This is not rational, but of course it is not about reason.

Perhaps this is St. Francis of Assisi's perception of the world. The world in which he lived was different to ours. Brother sun shone down on it, sister moon lit up the pilgirms' path at night and brother fire kept them from the cold. By day brother wind fined down the surface of sister water and at the end of his journey the pilgrim met with the sister bodily death. The world of living creatures. Maybe, no wonder, that at the first ever manger during the first Bethlehem ritual embodiment, it was through the famous infant miracle that those present saw the creation of the new age.

---

[22] This sentence together with the whole inspiration to use Paul VI. Missal I have found at www.petrapavel.cz and I am grateful to the authors.

We no longer perceive that as such. We know from school that our sun is a mixture of hydrogen and helium shaped into a sphere by gravitation and in which proton-proton fed reactions take place. These thermonuclear reactions are trying to split the sphere, while at the same the gravity compresses the gas atoms back again; we see the compromise in the sky. There is no reason to wave at a burning sphere. However wandering alone through the Andes gave me many an opportunity to reflect on this. I had many reasons to ponder this during my lone journey through the Andes. The Argentine flag has a yellow sun drawn in its middle, the same way as animists would see it with a nose, eyes and a mouth, the Uruguayan flag has it too. Paying with the Argentine pesetas, the same chubby sun with human features is ironically smiling at me.

Is it possible that the Argentinians can see something different to us? I wondered. How is it possible that we cannot even agree on what we can see in the sky every day?

During New Year celebrations we try to demonstrate the primordial chaos through our exuberant drinking, no longer realising why we treat the last day of the year with alcoholic intoxication.

THE INTERCONNECTED VESSELS
OF THE WORLD

———————————————

I.

We no longer say that if a man sins, all the carp
in the Brno dam die. However, according to the
Bible it is surprisingly true. Man is connected
to the land he lives on, man's sin and holiness
are also somehow projected onto nature. It was
only us in the West, who separated the history of
man from the history of nature. In line with our
understanding, nature functions independently
of human activity and during the floods in Bang-
ladesh or volcanic eruption in Iceland, we no
longer ask questions about what these events

should be telling us. Natural disasters are ethically neutral to us. In short, they took place and that was that.

For the Jews, on the other hand, history and nature are one. The common sin is also reflected in nature, in the same way as a blessing would be. After Adam and Eve's failure in Eden, God symptomatically says to them:

> *"Because you listened to your wife and ate from the tree about which I commanded you, 'You must not eat of it,' "Cursed is the ground because of you; through painful toil you will eat of it all the days of your life. It will produce thorns and thistles for you, and you will eat the plants of the field. By the sweat of your brow you will eat your food until you return to the ground, since from it you were taken; for dust you are and to dust you will return."*[23]

Cursed is the ground because of you, man sins and the consequences will be the earth producing only thorns and thistles for him. We would no longer say it like this. We understand sin as our personal failure, and frankly, it has nothing to do

---

[23] Genesis 3,17-19. (NIV)

with anyone else, people or beasts. This concept is accommodated by the location of the confession booth being the corner of the church, where the whispers of private confession between the penitent and the priest take place. However, according to the third chapter of Genesis, the earth is cursed because of Adam's sin. The man 'Adam' and the Earth 'adama' are connected to each other. After Abel's murder, God speaks to Cain in the same spirit:

> *"Now you are under a curse and driven from the ground which opened its mouth to receive your brother's blood from your hand. When you work the ground, it will no longer yield its crops for you. You will be a restless wanderer on the earth."*[24]

It appears that the earth has some peculiar sensitivity to the way humans treat one another and to the relationship between man and God. Human behaviour and the condition of the earth are connected to each other, and the ground will no longer yield its strength to Cain. The murder is no violation of some *ad hoc* covenant between

---

[24] Genesis 4,11–12. (NIV)

God and man, but it is a sin against all of creation, against God and all his work and the ground itself responds to the murder. And one more quote, this time from Isaiah:

"The earth is defiled by its people; they have disobeyed the laws, violated the statues and broken the everlasting covenant. Therefore a curse consume the earth; its people must bear their guilt. Therefore earth's inhabitants are burned up, and very few are left. The new wine dries up and the vine withers; all the merrymakers groan."[25]

Man breaks the everlasting covenant and the new wine dries up. This is how the old Israelites perceive the world. We recognise a good or a bad year at the vineyard usually in connection with plenty of sunshine and warmth in September, or a lack of it. We are not keen on looking for other reasons. It is impossible to omit the text from Job's defense in which the ground cries out:

"if my land cries out against me and all its furrows are wet with tears, if I have devoured its

[25] Isaiah 24,5-7. (NIV)

yield without payment or broken the spirit of its tenants, then let briers come up instead of wheat and weeds instead of barley."[26]

Job uses the ground as his witness during his defence – if he has sinned indeed, may weeds come up instead of barley! Let's finish our short biblical excursion with the most powerful place in Hosea:

"There is only cursing, lying and murder, stealing and adultery; they break all bounds, and bloodshed follows bloodshed. Because of this the land mourns, and all who live in it waste away; the beasts of the field and the birds of the air and the fish of the sea are dying."[27]

This text could become the leading text of modern environmental ethics. Should curses and hypocrisy take over the earth, all of the earth's population, animals, birds and fish shall wither away, as a result. Therefore, the social sin also projects itself onto nature. If man does not

---

[26] Job 31,38–40. (NIV)
[27] Hosea 4,2–3. (NIV)

live in peace with God, he cannot be at peace with the earth either. Nature is not a passive platform for the drama of our salvation, but rather an active participant – on one hand, punishing at God's command, and on the other, sending ravens with water and meat to Elijah. We would hardly perceive the world this way. Still, is the Old Testament not more right than we would usually like to admit? In 2006, the freshwater cetacean was declared functionally extinct in China. Clearly its extinction may not be linked to any esoteric curse or hypocrisy at the opposite end of China, but it is conclusively linked to the pollution of the river Yangtze and the pollution is still somehow linked to human indifference, lack of interest or selfish mercenary reasons, which links to human sin markedly. In this case, we can say with absolute ease that the extinction of the freshwater cetacean and human behaviour are somehow connected.

II.

We read similar stories in the New Testament. The Prodigal Son says to his father that he has sinned *"against heaven and against you"*[28].

---

[28] Luke 15,18. (NIV)

The sin is outlined not only vertically to the Father but also horizontally to other people.

If we were to take seriously Paul's picture of the church as a body, then it would be plausible to say that if one organ malfunctions, the whole body is suffering and the whole man ends up in hospital. However, the opposite is also true. One's holiness becomes the wealth of all, and within the interconnected vessels of the world a saint draws people to himself and somehow even sanctifies the landscape around him. When Jesus prepares for his public appearance in the wilderness, the Gospel of Mark states that *"he was with the wild animals, and angels attended him."*[29] Josef Ratzinger comments on this text:

"The wilderness – the opposite of the garden – becomes the place of reconciliation and healing; the wild animals representing the most definite threat to man through the rebellion against creation and the power of death, become friends like in Eden. Peace is re-established."[30]

---

[29] Mark 1,13. (NIV)

[30] Ratzinger, J., *Ježíš Nazaretský.* Barrister & Principal, Brno, 2007, p. 32.

It is striking, to say the least, how many legends portray saints and their warm relationship with animals. Certainly, Saint Francis and his many stories featuring lambs, kids and all domestic livestock, the robin redbreast which settled in the fraternal community, the donated tench which the saint set free and out of gratitude the fish circled his boat. On one occasion, Francis rebukes swallows during his sermon, not to disturb him with their chirping, and on another occasion, the animals gather around Francis and his monks out of their own will. When Francis meets the dreaded wolf of Gubbio, which is a danger to people, the saint reminds him of his place in the ecosystem and sure enough, the wolf obeys. The Franciscan Saint Anthony preaches to the fish that poke their heads out of the water as they listen (and that is remarkable for a biologist). His namesake Saint Anthony the Hermit, successfully rebukes the wild animals not to destroy the crop in his modest garden in Ireland, on his way through the forest the squirrels will be jumping into Saint Colombian's tunic, and in Russia the Orthodox Saint Seraphim of Sarov will befriend the bears. Before we dismiss these devout stories as implausible legends, it is worth noting that they are found in the hagiographies of different times and different geographical locations. Are they really so irrelevant? Providing man does not live in peace with Earth and God, what happens when man does begin to live in peace with God? Even today, do we not sometimes see how both the domestic and the wild animals recognise a kind man?

In modern medicine we understand disease in its molecular form, as a bacterial attack or viral infection and we perceive nature as the surroundings somewhere outside our window, as an environment that has not got much to do with us. As well as this, our various reflections and essays on natural conservation occasionally leave us with the impression that we stand alone, then comes some high wall, and finally beyond the city walls there is nature that is to be protected by us in the same way as we would protect a stamp collection.

I believe that is not how it is. We are a part of nature, not outside of it. The word 'health' has got the same root as the word 'whole', and 'holy'. Do we really think that we can be completely healthy and happy inside broken families, broken relationships and broken nature, with no definite repercussions for us?

In *The Outcry of Mute Things*,[31] the last text before his death (1993), Hans Jonas draws attention to the three parallels between the biblical message and the current state of the world. The Bible speaks about the original sin, universal to all mankind, the ecological crisis having a similar effect on both the poor and the rich on all continents. Furthermore, the Bible points to the fact that we are all sinners, the current crisis somewhat convinces us that in the ecological sense, all of us are 'sinners'. Finally, the Bible signals the Last Judgement at the end of time and warns about the possibility of hell. At present, concludes Jonas, we are heading for ecological hell without any 'supernatural' intervention. The fact that vines wither and fish in the sea are dying out, that dead Red-winged Blackbirds fall from the sky and the freshwater cetacean disappeared from the Earth, does not necessarily have to be in connection to some 'supernatural', bewitched divine intervention, it could be a logical and predictable consequence of a population's values in a certain area. Man's mind leaves an imprint

---

[31] Jonas, H., *Mortality and Morality. A Search for the Good after Auschwitz.* Northwestern University Press, Evanston, Illinois, US, 1996, p. 201–202.

on the landscape in which we live, giving it shape and making it in his image. Somebody must have made the decision that waste is going to be poured into rivers and that within ethical consideration, industrial boom will take center stage in the development of the region to the detriment of the clean river. In my country, this could be the landscape around Horni Jiretin, which reflects the soul of those in charge: extract and sell.

The destruction of nature democratically affects all the inhabitants of the Earth. Due to the flow of air through our global village, my car fumes affect all the inhabitants of the Earth equally, the transgression of one is a concern for the whole community, the holiness of one is the salvation of all. We are united in one large ecosystem of the world, where the church must play its part of salt or yeast, or whatever we want to call it, and to the traditional obligation of a Christian to God, fellow men and one's self, the fourth obligation is added: the obligation to the Earth, which we were given to govern.

III.

Modern evolutionary biology has changed the Darwinian paradigm of natural selection quite dramatically. Charles Darwin and many later generations of biologists assumed that evolution works according to the principle that children are born to parents with slight differences and nature itself selects the fittest. Therefore, from the rabbit offsprings 'on offer', those with the fastest legs run away from the fox, those with the thickest fur survive harsh winters, and those with the sharpest eyesight are able to spot the flying hawk in time. The fox, winter and hawk all serve as determining factors, getting rid of the weak and diseased, leaving the best to survive and multiply. Thus, the environment did not make the change, but merely chose it. One could picture the environment as a lock with a number of keys prepared in advance; the most successful at unlocking, survive. The original breeders followed exactly the same method. Breeding greyhounds for speed, they selected only the best from each litter and crossbred these again only with similarly fit puppies, and so on. Darwin came to the realisation that the breeder and nature always only select from the variations on offer. As it is said, *the organism is proposing and the environment is disposing.*

The question that biologists have asked (and the one I sometimes ask my students) is as follows:

if I held any kind of fertilised egg in my hand, perhaps a fertilised bird or crocodile egg, and if I knew all its proteins in detail, phospholipids, DNA, hormones, vitamins and any other substances contained within, if I knew in detail all the atoms and their special positions within the fertilised egg, would I be able to determine what comes out of it? So, in the distant future, providing I am able to convert all the information about the egg into electrical form and pour it into the computer, would I see the image of the given animal on the screen?[32]

Some students say 'yes' with hesitation.

The catch comes in our understanding of the word 'development', its meaning resembles the way we used to develop photographs in the darkroom not so long ago. My childhood memory: a dark red bulb, an enlarger, father slowly counting from twenty-one, twenty-two, twenty-three, little plastic bowls and the smell of fixative. The exposed photograph placed in the developer and an image soon emerging on the white paper, then

---

[32] Gilbert, S. F., Epel, D., *Ecological Developmental Biology. Integrating Epigenetics, Medicine and Evolution.* Sinauer Associates, Inc. Sunderland, Massachusetts, USA, 2009, p. 404.

into water it goes, then into the fixative and at the end back into water. To this day I reminisce the miracle. At times one understands the evolution of nature in the same way, completely in the spirit of Jurassic Park where DNA from a dinosaur is placed into an ostrich egg and a tiny dinosaur is born. The environment has a very passive role here, it only 'brings to surface' the program already encoded into the DNA long ago. The developer is not able to add or take away from a photograph, it only enables the holiday scene to become visible. Therefore, if I had the entire DNA code in my hand, in theory I should be able to read the final image of the organism, similarly to the instructions for use – screw it together and the job is done.

Today we believe that this is not how it works.

Currently we understand the environment as a much more prominent player. Some facts have been known to us since long ago. For example, when alligators lay eggs, much depends on the incubation temperature, when it comes to the gender of the animal. It works like this, gender is determined within a certain range of temperature, between 31–35°C in the case of the alligator. Males are born when the temperature reaches 33°C. Females are born when the temperature reaches either extremity. The temperature between 32°C and 34°C results in a fifty-fifty chance for both genders. Therefore, here the mere temperature during which the embryo starts to develop determines the gender of the newborn! Already the idea of the environment as a photo developer begins to crumble. This remarkable way of determining the gender of crocodiles could prove to be advantageous in some circumstances, but has its great disadvantages too. To this day, we are not exactly sure what caused the extinction of dinosaurs 65 million years ago. We know that at that time, a great asteroid hit the Yucatán Peninsula in Central America. What happened next, nobody knows exactly. It is assumed that a great tsunami followed. It is estimated that an impact on this scale could trigger volcanic activity worldwide.[33] A great crater from that time was found in the Ukraine. It is possible that the entire planet was bombarded by a meteor shower. Some scientists say that a great cloud of steam and ash covered

---

[33] Levin, H., *The Earth Through Time.* 9 ed. John Wiley & Sons, INC. Hoboken, NJ., 2009, p. 456-459.

the Earth and possibly no photosynthesis took place for many years. Due to the fact that no sun beams were able to reach the Earth, the Earth was most probably very cold. Or otherwise it could have been the complete opposite, the Earth was perhaps dark and hot. And so on. The most peculiar thing about it all is the fact that the groups we would not have expected to survive, have done so without any loss and vice versa the groups considered by us as widespread and invulnerable, vanished. Dinosaurs inhabited a number of different habitats and they were all around the Earth and yet they did not survive, becoming completely extinct. On the contrary, other species and families of organisms, we would maybe place our bet on as to their inability to withstand the change in their living conditions, crossed the border of Cretaceous/Paleogene periods more or less without a loss. The thermal gender determination could serve as a mosaic puzzle. If the gender of the newborn is merely determined by the temperature of the environment, it is very easy to imagine that dinosaurs (providing their gender was determined by temperature) could only bear offspring of the same gender during the long period of thermal pollution. Despite the fact that turtle gender is also determined by temperature, it is speculated that due to their ability to store sperm for a long time they would have been able to get through the catastrophic events quite well.

The second problem is very modern, regarding environmental activism. In our genuine effort to save a certain kind of crocodile or turtle, we collect their eggs and grow them in an incubator and in the end, satisfied with the number of young animals we managed to breed, we finally released them into the wild, failing to realise that because of the stable temperature of incubation we only bred individuals of the same gender. Similarly, if we only protect a small beach area where the eggs are naturally buried, we stand a large chance of only saving one gender.

The development does not necessarily have to be influenced by temperature alone, but also by the presence of one's enemies and one's allies. Breeding the *Hyla Chrysoscelis* tadpoles in a pond free of the predator dragonfly larva results in their long and slim shape.[34] Provided the larva are

---

[34] Gilbert, S. F., Epel, D., *Ecological Developmental Biology. Integrating Epigenetics, Medicine and Evolution.* Sinauer Associates, Inc. Sunderland, Massachusetts, USA, 2009, p. 26–33.

present in the pond, the tadpoles would be more muscular with a bright red tail. It is assumed that a more developed tail provides the tadpoles with greater speed and its colour intimidates the enemy. Now, listen closely. The same result would be achieved with an aquarium full of tadpoles by pouring in water in which the predator larva had spent time swimming about. It is certain that this is due to the chemicals, formally called kairomones, that the tadpoles are able to detect and adjust their pattern of evolution. Normally, the biblical desert locust *Schistocerca gregaria* is wingless, inconspicuously green and solitary, providing it has enough access to food. When food is in short supply, the locusts migrate to places where it is still possible to find some green leaves and this is when things start to happen. Mere mechanical touches of their femur ('thighs', the part of the body the locust uses to chirp) as the locusts crawl over one another, result in the wing growth and elongation of the body during their next molt. It would be to the same effect if we repeatedly used a small brush to stroke these body parts. The smell of the other locusts will cause the change in colour from green to bright red during the following molt. The colour will no longer serve as a camouflage but rather as striking and deterrent. Behaviour also changes. The solitary individuals form a large community, taking off and … the rest we can read about in the Bible.

And now, hot off the press: It turns out that once in a while something very peculiar takes place. Should the environment allow for a particular body shape for long enough, generation after generation, this final form becomes genetically fixed! We talk about the so called heterozygous,[35] change of rule. The example is evident and surprising. In spring *Aglais urticae*, small tortoiseshell butterflies, appear in large numbers all over the country. We have come across it many times throughout our lives but perhaps we did not recognise it. It has long since been known that when one refrigerates the chrysalises or cultivates them using a higher temperature, the final wing colour is clearly affected. Should one cultivate the chrysalises of this butterfly using a higher temperature, a form never seen in this

---

[35] Gilbert, S. F., Epel, D., *Ecological Developmental Biology. Integrating Epigenetics, Medicine and Evolution.* Sinauer Associates, Inc. Sunderland, Massachusetts, USA, 2009, p. 372-391.

part of the world emerges. Naturally, according to one's expectations, one finds the exact wing form on the specimen of this butterfly in Sardinia and Sicily. This is not surprising, as here in nature the same process from the experiment is carried out, with a slightly warmed cooker in an otherwise cold country. On the other hand, it is surprising that the Sardinian tortoiseshell butterflies have their colours genetically fixed! They do not look the way they do because of a lower or higher temperature, but because of their genetic code. What probably happened after generations of tortoiseshell butterflies developing in a warm climate, the influence of the environment caused the identical wing pattern to re-emerge, until it finally became genetically fixed. Thus, the appearance of Sardinian tortoiseshell butterflies is no longer influenced by the temperature in which the chrysalis was formed. Therefore, the environment not only chooses the existing change, but is also responsible for the direct creation of this change!

This significantly complicated introduction has its own very important philosophical impact. The environment does not only run the programme which is coded in one's DNA, it is also its creator. One's allies and enemies, the country in which one lives, the Earth which one is a part of, influences much more than ever imagined. The environment is not just there to nourish in order to facilitate development, the environment is one's sculptor, allowing changes to be passed onto future generations. Without the rest of the living, one would not be oneself. Without one's allies and enemies, one would not become whom one is. We are all interconnected.

From this thought, a very important argument regarding the protection of the environment is formed. We should not protect the environment just because it gives us oxygen, coal or wood for building, but rather because we are a part of it. There is no wall between man and nature. Maybe in the same way the presence of a dragonfly larva influences the colouring of a tadpole, or the presence of others causes the growth of wings, perhaps with a much stronger influence than we could ever imagine, one is influenced by the environment, the rocks, forests, animals, people who God somehow sends one's way, experiences and unexpected meetings, allies and enemies and all the good people one is surrounded by. On the other hand, what one says, how one acts, the way one is, influences one's friends in return and influences the nature that is one's home. The intuition of natives suggesting everything is interconnected, that we are a part of the power curves of the universe, is perhaps more profound than we ever thought. We must protect nature in the same way as we protect our own body, our own hands, our own heart, because every living thing is interconnected in a network of relationships, in the fibres of life. Saint Francis of Assisi's concept of animals and flowers as being little brothers and sisters is given further support from a very unusual side. One is connected to one's brothers, 'big' and 'small', they are all somehow a part of oneself. When Saint Paul refers to the church as a body in which each Christian is a cell, a tissue or an organ in this shared body, perhaps we could take this more literally than we have done so far. Paul explains that if one of your body parts is suffering, the whole body suffers. The blood that supplies the body is the blood of the Holy altar, the head of the body is Christ. The holiness of one is the holiness of all, the sin of one is also the possession of the whole fellowship. Or to put it differently using the colourful comparison made by the saint fathers, seeds of Eucharists sprouted on many a little field of different mountaintops, to be later gathered together, beaten, grounded, mixed with water (here, the fathers refer to the baptismal water), put into the oven (the fire of the Holy Spirit) and the end result was bread – the Eucharist. In a similar way, we should also be connected, not only as separate shoots on different mountains, not only as different seeds in one basket, but rather we should form one body of one Eucharist bread bound by water and fire.

IV.

It is a paradox that today more than ever we are aware of how influential interaction with other organisms is during the process of making a new organism. Symbiosis, live-together, can become symbiogenesis[36] when, for example, long term advantageous cooperation influences the emergence and form of the new species. A long time ago, two bacteria joined together to create the first eukaryotic cell, then these cells began to live together and multicellular organisms came into

---

[36] Margulis, L., Sagan, D., *Acquiring Genomes. A Theory of the Origins of Species.* Basic Books, NY, 2002, p. 11–19.

being, from which we will eventually be formed, and mitochondria in our body are a reminder of this ancient symbiosis, for mitochondria 'tiny cells within a cell', which create energy in us, used to be living free as alpha proteobacteria a long time ago. Today they are not able to exist independently, they live satisfied inside of our cells to both our and their benefit. If one organism lives inside the other, mitochondria within us, *or whether we have become them*, that is a question of philosophy.

We are not exactly sure where to place lichens, because lichens are certainly not plants, nor fungi or algae. A lichen is a certain form of live-together of algae[37] and fungus (if I want to avoid emotionally charged words like cooperation or parasitism). While algae or cyanobacteria forming lichens can still live independently, fungus no longer can and a lichen as a unit becomes a new type of organism. Sometimes, when a certain type of lichen lives in darkness for a long time, the fungus grows larger,

---

[37] The photosynthesising part of a lichen is formed either by algae (genus Trebouxia, Pseudo Trebouxia, Trentepohlia), or cyanobacteria (Nostoc). These four genera form 90 % of all lichens.

consuming the algae. Other times, if a lichen spends a long time in water and light at the same time, the fungus 'drowns' and algae grow in its place. It depends on the conditions.[38]

Gastropoda *Elysia viridis* is a close relative of our garden slugs, but *Elysia* is green because it consumes algae and also their chloroplasts. Chloroplasts not only survive in the body of the gastropoda, but even continue photosynthesis. Therefore, just like plants this sea gastropoda does not have to consume food, providing he absorbs enough sunlight, taking care of the glucose required. This way, Elysia benefits from the advantageous connection between animals and plants. Similarly, coral reefs in warm seas are formed by colonial species of corals, in which mutualistic photosynthetic algae live and offer the photosynthesis products to the corals that they would otherwise die without.

During my trek through the Argentine savannahs, I very much enjoyed stopping by the giant anthill *Atta vollenweideri*, resembling a generously designed children's playground,

---

[38] Margulis, L., Sagan, D., *Acquiring Genomes. A Theory of the Origins of Species.* Basic Books, NY, 2002, p. 20.

and I was thinking about how our concept of biological species is too limited, disjointed and discrete. The *Atta* ants and also the *Acromyrmex* ants cut green leaves which they carry to the underground part of the anthill. Here they cut them into 1-2 mm pieces with their mandibles, chewing and then spraying them with a solution of antibiotics and disinfectants against bacteria and unwanted kinds of fungi. They put them carefully into their underground garden and cover them with a little ball of fungus mycelia of the genus *Leucocoprinus gongylophorus*. The ants also excrete the solution onto the garden, which is a growth hormone aiding the growth of the mycelia of this fungus. Over the course of 24 hours the fungus grows, covering the leaves, and its hyphae with hyphal swellings called gongylidia will serve as the food for the ants' larva. Perhaps a garden is not a suitable word, its depth could be three to six meters and myrmecologists use bulldozers to successfully investigate. Though the fungus might belong to the basidiomycota (where our boletus or common mushroom also belong) the ants never allow it to form spores. That is why until today it has been debated where exactly this fungus systematically belongs.[39] During her nuptial flight, as a part of her dowry, the future ant queen also takes some of this fungus mycelium into her special little pocket. The fungus is no longer able to grow on its own and fully relies on its cohabitation with the ants. To complete the story, the digestion of cellulose from the cut up leaves is shared inside of the fungus by several kinds of bacteria and yeast. Thus, the life of the fungus and the ants is inseparably joined, one would not survive without the other. One organism shapes the other.

For the survival of their kind, many plants need insect pollinators and on the other hand, the pollinators would not survive without nectar. Where would bees be without wildflowers and flowers without bees! Sometimes the relationship is so close that one particular kind of plant needs one particular kind of insect, for example a certain kind of orchid needs a certain kind of lichen, and both of these otherwise unrelated kinds progress through centuries in tandem, inseparable. And

---

[39] Hölldobler, B., Wilson, E. O., *The Ants.* Springer-Verlag, Berlin, Heidelberg, London, Paris, Tokyo, Hong Kong, 1990, p. 596–608.

we can go on: the life necessity of orchids is the connection of its roots to a friendly fungus, otherwise they will not survive. And so forth.

Thanks to global warming, some types of trees in our hemisphere started to spread northwards. Many of them would not be able to do this fast enough if their seeds were only falling down to the ground without the help of wind, birds or animals dispersing them further.

The relationship between man and his gut flora would be a similar story; one cannot survive without the other. Vitamins B and K are making us exactly these microorganisms and we cohabit in a quiet and usually unconscious unity with these microbes inside us. An organism is a community of players that are dependent on each other in different ways, in the same way that the whole ecosystem is a community of co-dependent players.[40] Pollinating insects would not survive without nectar and flowers would not multiply without pollinators. The roots of probably all plants rely on mykorrhiza, bound to fungi, where the fungi help absorb minerals

[40] Margulis, L., Sagan, D., *Acquiring Genomes. A Theory of the Origins of Species.* Basic Books, NY, 2002, p. 18.

from the soil and in return receive products of photosynthesis.

Then if we deny the mitochondria in our body the status of a 'kind', and if we give lichens individual names, we should also give a single status of an individual kind to the united *Atta* ants and *Leucocoprinus* fungi. The message is very important: sometimes there are two kinds of organisms completely dependent on one another, sometimes not as dependent, but a certain degree of dependence always exists.

Perhaps our whole concept of 'kind' is somewhat wrong. There are not individual kinds, there is Life, one without the other is lost. *Atta* ants would die without their fungi and *Leucocoprinus* fungi without its ants, and a man would die exactly like that without his gut bacteria.

And the matter could be generalised by saying that no organism can survive without help from and cooperation with other organisms, no kind in the world could survive on its own. That is also true about man. We are also formed by a number of interactions with life in us and around us. We are a part of nature, not outside of it. Symbiosis influences the shape and properties of organisms and thus becomes symbiogenesis.

V.

When one thinks about things that are working well, and about our so called pastoral success, one asks oneself, what anonymous granny has been praying for us and where may she be, because we are interconnected like water in joined vessels. Wenceslas, Ludmilla, Adalbert, Constantine and Methodius used to walk this land, on the same Czech soil as we walk now, and they were praying for us, in the same way as my parents pray for me, and my grandparents, and my great grandparents. We are standing on the shoulders of our ancestors and now it is our turn to pray for our children, our grandchildren, our great grandchildren whom we will not reach within our life span and will not get to meet – within the interconnected vessels of this world.

A long time ago, when I was about sixteen years old, we were travelling by boat on the Vltava river and on the way from Studena Vltava we visited Vyssi Brod monastery. After a while, I stopped listening to the tour guide and was sucked in by the atmosphere of the place, the monastery's genius loci. At the time I was under the intense impression that the serious faces of the paintings were full of secrets, longing and even unspoken effort, that the monks and abbots from the canvases were trying to tell us something important, that they did not have their portraits painted out of vanity, but in order to let us know, crossing the abyss of centuries to make us aware, that here at this very place they were praying for us, were happy about something and worried about something, and that they were praying for us, the generations to come, that they are leaving us a legacy that could be seen only indirectly through the beauty of the stone archways and sharp steeples and that when they were carving the stone they were thinking of God and of us. We were walking through the church and I felt that the monks stood there with us. I believe that God takes every prayer seriously. I believe in the prayers of our ancestors, I believe in the prayers of all the Czech saints, I believe in the prayers of the sick and the old, I believe in the prayers of little children. I believe that when I celebrate The Holy Mass, the church of the Saints, the fellowship of monks from Vyssi Brod and all other such fellowships are standing around the altar. I believe that when I celebrate the Holy Mass, I do so in the name of those who have not been born yet, in the name of the future saints, in the name of the grandchildren and great grandchildren who are to come and whose coming we are preparing.

VI.

In its intuition, the church has in great respect contemplative monasteries that are in practical terms useless to the nation. Monks could be working in hospitals, they could be responsible for education, they could awaken hearts through their own example within the local parish area or be kind parents, and instead monks do nothing, nothing visible that is, they only work for their living and pray for the lands in which they live, for the global village of the world. Yet their invisible task is far more important than the visible work of all the others.

During our camp for secondary school students, every year without exception something extraordinary takes place. Some settle their business through the sacrament of reconciliation after many years, for some the decision to get baptised begins to emerge, and the whole time I am thinking about the anonymous grannies in old people's homes and nuns in contemplative monasteries. We are connected to each other, like the blood that connects one body, like the threads of the Church Body. We, the camp leaders, are only prop managers on the world's stage.

SAINT THERESE OF LISIEUX'S DILEMMA

During RE lessons, I read this text to my students from time to time and then I asked them what they thought. The reading is from none other than 'The Story of A Soul'.

There is a sister in our community with a special talent that makes me dislike everything about her. Her behaviour, her words and her character seemed very unpleasant to me. Still, she is a saint, and member of a religious order, who is surely very dear to the Lord God. This is why I was not willing to give into the natural antipathy that I have been experiencing, but rather told myself that love does not depend on feelings, but on action. Therefore, I tried to do for this sister what I would do for a person I love the most (...) I felt that this was pleasing to Jesus because there has not yet been a creator that would not be pleased to be praised for what he has created, and Jesus the creator of souls is happy when we do not stop at the outward appearance but we delve deeper into the inner sanctuary, which he has chosen as his dwelling, and we admire its beauty. I was not happy just to be praying for the sister, who cost me so much strife. I tried to serve her in every way possible, and when I was tempted to answer her unkindly, I settled for a smile, the sweetest smile, and a change of conversation. (...) When my battle became too severe, I ran away like a deserter. As the sister was completely unaware of my real feelings towards her, she remained ignorant of my behavioral motive. She was convinced that I found her character pleasant. Once, after her recovery, she told me with an expression of satisfaction on her face, something like this: 'Could you tell me sister Therese of Jesus' child, what draws you to me so? Every time you look at me

I can see you are smiling.' Oh, what I was drawn by, was Jesus, hidden in her soul... (...) I replied that I am smiling because I am glad to see her (of course I did not add that it was meant from a spiritual point of view).[41]

So what? Was St. Therese dissembling or not? If everyone around us acted like this, we would find ourselves on the set of a horror movie; the people sitting around me are smiling, do they really love me or are they pretending out of Christian love? What if I am some particularly repulsive, obnoxious, unbearable (high school students have thoughts like this from time to time) individual and the rest talk to me only because of their Christian compassion, the friends around me trying their best to put on a face and pretend that all is well? How do we go about friendship, after all? Do we really love each other? Do the girls around me really like me, or am I surrounded by smiling Christian women everywhere and I am no longer sure what real friendship is, nor a front? When I take a critical look at myself in the mirror,

---

[41] Svatá Terezie z Lisieaux, *Autobiografické spisy (Dějiny duše).* Nakladatelství tiskárny Vimperk, 1991, p. 217-218.

I wonder could someone love something like this, at all? There are moments when I even feel guilty about the air that I breathe (said one of my students) and most of the time my confidence is non-existent. What if all of my friends sigh a sigh of relief. When I leave the room, and behind my back they send compassionate looks to the person. Who is speaking to me at the time? And when I receive an invite to a birthday party, is it because as Christian people you want to invite the sad, poor and limping of this world, or do you feel as good as I do when I am around you? Is there a group of saintly, sweet smiling Thereses for whom a conversation with me requires great effort, as I am living under the illusion that I am loved? And the man who finished his conversation with me so abruptly, was it because his battle with me was too severe? Are my friends going to tick a 'good deed' box in their scout diary, for giving me five minutes of their time today? Am I able to read into the real reason for the presents that I receive? And why am I getting encouraging texts? Is it always better not to concentrate on what people are saying but why they are saying it, and what if the rest are certain that by wasting time speaking to me, they are doing a good deed? I, surrounded by all kinds of good samaritans who come down to me from their height and pretend to be interested in me, willing to hear me out, perhaps even give advice and even pay the pub owner the two denary for me.

Perhaps then it is better to make it clear to my classmates whom I consider close and whom not, with whom I want to be friends and with whom not. The friend request on Facebook: accept or ignore. It is better to have true friendship as well as true enmity, transparent relationships without pretence, a situation where all things are clearly laid out on the table. At least I would know where I stand. One copes better with indifference, being ignored and open enmity, rather than compassion.

However, it is not always that easy. Every one of us goes through moments when we prefer to be on our own, but a friend comes to talk to us and we decide to talk, because despite our aversion, we consider our friendship worth keeping. The reason for this is our desire not to stop at the outer appearance, during this less enjoyable moment, in our pursuit to discover this person's inner being. To love the other person, if not for who they are but for who they could become, to love the light in them, that has once been given to them and which hopefully still flickers somewhere inside of them, not to stop at the surface but get inside, despite the fact that now, today or tomorrow we will still not be able to stand that person. If a man can perceive this, then it is a sign that we love one another, and in the other I could perhaps love not his actual words and actual unpleasant, ugly and perhaps objectively bad deeds, but the light inside of them, their 'I', the image of God in them, 'I' that is perhaps much more real than the skin on their face, their actual words and present deeds. The fact that right now, they are doing badly, does not necessarily have to mean that the mistake is in my neighbour, but rather I learn something important about myself and my limitations. I think that this is what St. Therese wanted to say, and I believe that her love is much more honest and deeper than our present sympathy to words and the face's appearance. To pass the whirlwind of emotions to the deeper levels of our soul, where it is not windy and the little flame is peaceful, to the depths of the sea, where the ripples on its surface are far away, unnoticeable and unimportant. Great philosophers say that it is not possible to learn about a thing as it truly is. We perceive it only using our imperfect senses, making a mental picture of it in our mind, *fainomenon*, but the true reality of something. In objective terms, *noumenon*, we might never find out. It is similar with us. We love or hate our picture of other people, not who they really are. The reason for love or hatred is in us (not in them). If we are able to look inside, we see the picture of God, light, which reflects the Creator of the soul. *And Jesus, the creator of the soul is happy, when we do not stop at the outer appearance, but when we go deeper into the inner sanctuary, which he has chosen for his dwelling, and we admire its beauty.*[42]

[42] Svatá Terezie z Lisieaux, *Autobiografické spisy (Dějiny duše).* Nakladatelství tiskárny Vimperk, 1991, p. 217-218.

ET DIMITTE NOBIS
DEBITA NOSTRA

———————————

Not so long ago, I was approached by a Catholic periodical to write about the current state of priesthood, the loneliness of priests, burnout and how to prevent it. The text is still a work in progress and should be intellectual enough.[43] However, beneath the surface a different story is emerging. It is the one I present to you now. The parts all relate to priestly ordination and God.

———————————

[43] Later, the article was published in Perspektivy 13/2010.

I.

The first is of when I gave my lecture in K. and later went to spend the night in Lechovice, only to drive back to the remote part of the country in the morning. To attend the funeral of a friend, a fellow priest, who was a victim of a bad train accident. The good Catholics of K. were more than willing to share what really happened and explain that it was not nearly as accidental, that there was a relationship, a woman, a child and a whole lot of other things and that my friend the priest in his desperation left to be killed on the tracks. He could not see any other solution to his double life. Later, I found the train driver's witness account of what happened. He describes how he saw a person standing there and how he put his breaks on, breaking hard and that the person kept on standing there and never got out of the way. What really happened, I do not know, I only know what I have been told by the parishioners of K., and what I know from the train driver's witness account. I have not searched any further. It could have been the plot for a film.

I was driving home from K. and felt overcome by sorrow, great sorrow, and the silhouette of the figure standing in the dark on the train tracks was following me. I was heading for Lechovice thinking about all of us priests, and how we are dying one after another, and God willing through His mercy, in our weakness, we leave in time, to embrace marriage and family or else. We stay strong and suffer until death.

I was thinking about Honza P. and Honza M. and others, who used to be and no longer are with us, and driving fast on the motorway. My car slipped on the ice and flew over the barriers and then over the frozen hillside and the car began to spin, turning around several times repeatedly, like a spinning top and I broke the bumpers, doors, mirrors and landed on the frozen field in Pohorelice, two or three meters under the motorway, and when the car stopped spinning, I put on the breaks and got out of the car which had its lights on and the engine still running, and I never registered that I nearly killed myself.

I got out of the car thinking about my friend the priest who committed suicide, and I desperately wanted to call someone close, and so, I took my phone out of my pocket. And at that moment, I realised that there was nobody close to call, that I have many brothers and sisters, but in my scrupulous anxiety, there was nobody I could call on Friday at eleven at night and say that I have wrecked the car and my friend is dead and that I feel bad, and so I helplessly held the phone in my hand and knew that it was like in the song and that all my friends are asleep, asleep, asleep with their wives at home and there is no one in the world and when I closed my eyes, I saw the silhouette of the figure, standing on the train tracks, and I was begging him and pleading with him to move away, for God is above time, and I was kneeling down and crying as he stood there motionless. Only a little further down, the same silhouette of my dead friend stood on the train tracks with his head bowed down, waiting for the blow and somewhere a child was crying. This is the story about priesthood and its current state.

II.

The second story is a bit longer. A long time ago, I felt the world gained its meaning and flowers shivered as if made of silver, as everything in the world reassembled from chaos into a beautiful form, and at that very moment the universe was created, a great pain with its deadly force, yet it was worth it. I kept a diary and it was published as a book, based on a true story. God, I asked, does the universe exist because of us?

However, once I also experienced the opposite. The image shattered and individual pieces of the beautiful form were blown away by the great force of a powerful gale into nonexistence, and the flowers and birds disappeared and the sky folded in like a tent and only the pain remained. God, I asked again, slightly surprised, was it really supposed to be this way?

The presenter of the "News at Midnight" announced that astrophysicists had just calculated the future of the universe, and found out that the dark matter between the stars is greater than expected, and that according to the latest calculations the old and tired force of the Big Bang will not be able to sustain further expansion of the world. That afternoon, in Wenceslas Square, in front of the amazed crowds of people looking up with their binoculars, blackened pieces of glass and scientific guides, the entire universe came to a halt for a moment. At first imperceptibly, slowly and then faster and faster it began to contract and the redshift was replaced by the blueshift in response to the gravitational force of hatred pulling the entire world into singularity and all the globular clusters and galaxies started to come closer with no chance of turning back. The power of love in our story about humans was not enough to balance out the powers of hatred, for God, apart from His love, also needs our five loaves of bread, and when human love is nonexistent, the entire world pulls towards itself by devious silos forces of hatred, begins to draw in, until it shrinks into the initial chaos of nothingness. All this when hatred outweighs love, and fairy tales are wrong in what they say about the good conquering evil in the end, because the end is left open.

The thousand-head herds of the African plains, together with all the birds and fish, being sustained by love for so many years, died out in a split second and in a hurry the heavenly sail was folded away like a musty old cloth. What I am about to say now is not meant figuratively, but literally. I believe that to God, love is so important that He is able to create the entire universe with galaxies and quasars and globular clusters for the sake of two people, and that when our human love ceases to exist He could roll it all up like old plans, extinguish the stars and go home because the reason behind His creation is love. Every life has infinite value. The universe was created because of me. The universe was created because of you. The universe was created for the sake of every individual human being, because of every citizen on this planet, and when we stop loving, when we have no more love to give, its existence passes. How many times have we heard from the pulpits that human life has infinite value? The ability to think this through would finally lead us to earnestly value ourselves, our time and our prayers.

And so, we, the priests, like Arthur's knights, tread through the snowy plains under the silent sky with no sense of things in sight. Forgive us our trespasses, God, and forgive us, when from time to time, we humans, are unable to forgive.

PINK GOD

It would be beautiful to keep our childhood faith until adulthood, to believe in a flat Earth with the heavens above it, and to believe in heaven and the kind God who is in charge of everything. It would be beautiful to believe in the calm and great hierarchy of creation, in the wise God, in crisp white angels and god-fearing human-kind redeemed. To believe in the unchanging garden of nature, which was left to us by God on the sixth day. To believe that the world is six thousand years old and death came to it only through human sin. To believe that the fruit of prayer is the blessing of earthly possession, and that those faithful on Earth are doing well and those without God badly, that our minor suffering is the punishment for our minor sins, that a man is in fact good, and that when we are suffering, it is because we deserve it. To believe in a world in which our loving God is looking down over the heavens and people, full of love in a poetic set-up of the static and forever fixed universe of school children, where the border between Earth and the heavens is separated by only a transparent curtain. We were once taught this in our seminary: a man is standing in the middle of the imaginary sand dial, with the heavens and angels overhead and higher still, the everlasting God. There, beneath the man, the pyramid opens up, revealing all living things, animals, plants and the nonliving world of minerals and rocks. In the middle of all that is happening, intersecting the matter and the spiritual, at the top of the pyramid mass and at the bottom of the spiritual heaven stands a man, the centre of the world, lower than angels, higher than animals. There is good in every man and our minor sins are, in effect, acceptable and the good God will forgive us all in the end. I remember my mother telling me, a six-year-old boy, after my confirmation, that I have a lot of gold in heaven, and how I completely believed her without any hesitation. I am envious, very envious, of the fundamentalists with their faith in the young Earth, righteous God and the black and white world.

At some stage, sooner or later, a child loses his innocence. Suffering that befalls him will sometimes be justified and other times be very unfair, blind, make no sense, and seem cruel. I am sitting in the coffee shop with my friend drinking mulled wine as she tells me her story, matter-of-fact and without emotion. She was totally in love with a man, but she knew that she had no chance, that he never even noticed her, and her suffering seemed endless. One night, they were on the phone to each other, and during the conversation he declared his love for her, and that he had been suffering and suffering for months, thinking she had never even noticed him and that he stood no chance, word for word, he believed exactly the same as she did. All is said, explained and declared, a long telephone call with tears. That night, the man drove somewhere and died in a car crash. We were sipping our mulled wine, and matter-of-fact, without any emotion, my friend told me that since that moment, she finishes every sentence of Catechism and every sentence declaring her faith, using a comma instead of a full stop, followed by the word 'perhaps'.

We are living in one of a billion galaxies, on a tiny planet, which is seen from the distance of the universe as shaking from the explosions of warring sides, and which, from the depth of the universe, appears to be a bunch of thugs. We are not standing at the top of the pyramid, we are only one of the many branches of the ever-changing and pulsing life in the ever-developing, unstable universe. We are one kind out of the many possible species. The only thing that sets us apart from the others is the fact that we were the first to break through the curtain of ignorance. We became aware of ourselves, and began to make use of our double edged tool – the mind. And the minute we came to this realisation. We were given freedom, and together with the gift of love, we also opened ourselves up to hatred. We were the only ones whom God had given the gift of humility, and with it came the possibility of pride. Explosions overcame the green Earth and blue sky. While watching the news we could ask God, from time to time, if this was the way He intended for it to be. The good Catholics among us are trying to fit the pain of small children, the meaningless, unjust, and undeserved pain, into the glorious hierarchy of the universe with the angel choir and kind God. No matter what, we try to find an explanation and fit reality into our picture of the great heavenly theatre, often in a very clumsy way. I imagine God moulding us from the earth and then leaving us be, only to bear children in time and form a network of relationships, and as soon as that happens, we, the moulded figure, are knocked back down by God into non-existence, and only the torn remnants of relationships and pain remain. I remember when my sister-in-law died at the age of thirty-five and how after the funeral people were coming to us to reassure us that God is good, He knows what He is doing, and I was holding the hand of Sister anxiety in silence, and she was smiling sweetly at the ones condoling.

Another friend was telling me the story of her time as a young mother when her child contracted leukemia and how the doctors asked her to say goodbye six times in total, because there was no chance of recovery and her child would die. In the end, the child survived. The friend explained that the greatest torment was when Catholics were coming to her, explaining why she was going through all this.

It is a strange paradox: on one hand, God sends to man destructive natural catastrophes, earth-quakes, landslides and raging nature killing bad and good, children, girls and women, and on the other hand, the same God is called just and mer-ciful. Is that possible?

And we, just like Job once, are crying to the heavens and hear no reply.

A long time ago, Job's friends came to him to explain his situation, to give him advice and to let him know the state of things. To give his story the right treatment and mould it into a different story, the story of the almighty and merciful God. Today Job's story is repeated over and over again, and we are always available, us friends, to take the side we believe is God's side, and to try to justify the situation, to explain it, to give advice, to point out mistakes, and to fit today's story of suffering into the everlasting script of the loving godly Saviour. Perhaps we do not do this for the sake of today's Jobs, but for our own sake. We try to find an explanation for the unexplainable and for our own peace, preserve the image of the wise and kind Redeemer, trying to force the facts to rhyme with our vision of God. And we are mistaken when we call those who manage this, humble and deeply pious. Job used to be like this once in the first couple of paragraphs of his book, saying with exemplary humility *God has given, God has taken, blessed be his name.*[44] For the rest of the story, Job shouts in vain into the deaf and gloomy sky, where God makes a pact with the devil, letting him come up with more tests.

A woman came to my parish once and said that her young child had died that day. What can one possibly say to that? How can one possibly explain, clarify or encourage? Could you answer to man's suffering by giving a lecture? How can one reason with heartache? Soften the blow with arguments? Was I to slap the woman's shoulder and with priestly enthusiasm say: "Dear lady, well this is how it goes…?" Or were we to sing together "How wonderful must the love be…?"

I asked another friend of mine suffering from cancer whether my visits were not too tiring for her. No, she answered, the only thing that makes me tired are my friends who come to explain to

---

[44] Job 1,21. (NIV)

me. How they came to terms with my illness. At the time, it occured to me I had read this somewhere before.

I admit that God's ways are not my ways and that God's wisdom is all knowing and far supersedes my miniscule human reason. However, especially as far as cancer is concerned, I have a very strong feeling that death's arrow hits people absolutely at random, without selection, stochastically, good and evil, young and old, beautiful and less beautiful, new fathers and pregnant mothers who run the crazy race to give birth before death catches up with them. And often it is the mother together with the child who lose as the tumor comes faster than the due date. All of us Catholics have been in prayer battles, with the subsequent meeting over the coffin with the two bodies, the yellow autumn leaves and the ravens of Brno's cemetery are forever in my memory. It is only in fairy-tales that princes and their princesses live happily ever after. Could there possibly be any higher logic to this? From experience I say this is not the case.

To put it differently, sometimes a man finds himself in a situation that has nothing to do with him, he just happened to be there. One of his decisions could be very bad, but the other could be even worse. To do nothing is also very bad. Here, the very concept of good and evil collapses, together with the idea of justice and injustice. Like in the song, no promise can be kept or broken.

Perhaps it has also crossed our minds whether it was not possible to arrange things differently, when looking at Christ in the Garden of Gethsemane, overcome by terror and anxiety and sweating blood. Is the good God, who is love, so unappeasable that He has to save humankind from itself only through Christ's death, and where we would expect understanding and forgiveness, the act of mercy must be redeemed by human sacrifice?[45] Do we, the people who have connected our lives to Christ in one way or another, have to sweat blood from time to time, and in terror and anxiety, ask what our God is really like? The story of Job is repeated. Even today, amidst our suffering we hear that it is better this way, that God surely knows what He is doing, that our human reason is not able to decipher God's unpredictable ways,

---

[45] Jung, C. G., *Výbor z díla IV., Obraz člověka a obraz Boha.* Brno: Nakladatelství Tomáše Janečka, 2001, p. 371.

that it is necessary to bow down in deep piety before the work of God's never-ending mercy, and in the same way the poor girl from Nazareth did, we are to say our humble *fiat*, that in the end all is in order, and that we should actually rejoice and that we could even have joy in our hearts every hour of every day. Maybe today friends will come, as they did long ago to Job, and will try to stand up for their God, point out His wisdom and our sins, and they will want to become God's advocates against man.

Who is being defended by whom and who are they against? No, we are not trying to comfort others, we are above all trying to comfort ourselves, we are not trying to explain things to others, we are trying to silence ourselves with our own words, to persuade ourselves that our idea of kind God exists and must be valid, and at the same time somewhere inside we feel that we are trying to justify the unjustifiable. And so we try, in vain, to save our flat Earth and static world peace, the world without great suffering, watched over by God's kind eye of providence, and where things are kept in place.

We thought that God was just, but together with Job we have discovered that God is not like that.

And after this, standing in the fragments of our childlike picture of God, an adult faith can be born, faith of those who have thrown away the childlike faith and everything childish, faith that helped the chosen nation survive Auschwitz, the stubborn faith without any illusions, the dark, naked and cold faith, the faith in God almighty who is often unkind and unfair. Faith that is not afraid to ask what is hidden behind the concept of 'God'. Faith which despite all cruelty and all that God does in order to discourage us from believing in Him, will be together with Job shouting into the silent heavens, the Jewish *shema israel, adonai eloheinu, adonai echad.*

THE MOST COMMON ATHEIST MISCONCEPTIONS

A large number of my friends are atheists and now and again we talk faith, Christianity and things to do with the church. Over time I have noticed that independently of each other, my atheist friends sometimes share the same beliefs. Where they got them from, only God knows. As time went by, I made a list for my personal use, which later on I shared as the most common atheist misconceptions. Excuse my being ironic. However, before I start criticising something, perhaps the thing to do would be to read about it from a credible source.

Christians are people who live their lives according to the Ten Commandments

Only they don't. An atheist is surprised and appalled when he can see the lapse of individual Christians, and he complains that Christians preach water but drink wine, believing wrongly that to be a Christian means to live an exemplary and sin-free life according to the Ten Commandments.

It is not surprising that this is not the case. Christians are tempted in the same way as everyone else, with the same problems and the same failures. If an atheist notices that Christians do not live according to the Ten Commandments, he is right. The difference is perhaps in the fact that a Christian is, or should be, more aware of it, and the claim *'I have killed none, I have not robbed anybody, I live a good life'* could be heard more often from atheists than from Christians.

Sometimes we hear from the pulpit, that the only one in the history of the world who managed to live without sin and keep sharp ideal was Jesus Christ, however an atheist draws no conclusions based on this fact, and again and again he is surprised that Christians are unable to live without sin.

Christians think that they are
better than atheists

Surely not. Perhaps it is not necessary to oppose this nonsense, it is all related to what we have just discussed in the previous paragraph. An atheist visits a random church with its random mass where at the beginning he listens to the joint declaration *I confess to Almighty God and to you, that I have greatly sinned in my thoughts and in my words, in what I have done and in what I have failed to do, through my fault, through my most grievous fault*, and that it is enough for him. In debates, the existence of moral atheists and immoral Christians is always pointed out. Surprisingly, no atheist ever compares moral Christians with immoral atheists, yet both categories are represented in high numbers. A lot of atheists refuse to become Christians when they argue the failure of different Christian rulers, popes or priests, but surprisingly they refuse to leave the atheist 'group' following Hitler and Stalin's rule. Those who are stereotypically complaining about both the made up and real evil that the church has been responsible for in the past, could take a look at atheists and the world that surrounds them not doing any better but rather much worse, with either the same or poorer results. Sometimes atheists paint a picture of the world in which there are many good and noble organisations and together with them the black stain of the bad Catholic Church which is responsible for so much evil, as we often hear. Clearly that is wrong. Throughout history there has never been a human organisation with clean hands, no kingdom, no state, no organised structure, no political party. The only organisation that has survived the past two thousand years is the church, and it would be utterly surprising if this happened without sin. After all, that is not even possible! Contemplating the evil throughout history, we touch on something deep in man, independently of the organisation of which this or that king or general is a member. The history of China is not any more merciful than the history of Europe. Obviously there are no clear Christian roots, it is rather cruel with typical Asian callousness towards humans. Do we know of any noble, pure, non-problematic, non-religious or religious organisation? The history of Africa is not any better and our utter horror is prevented only due to the luck of scribes present on this continent throughout the past centuries. In this world, is there any non-corrupt and noble political party, any squeaky clean religious group or church, pure humanitarian organisation, any kind of humanitarian state, that would remain pure longer than one day?

As far as those known to us are concerned, above all, I believe that we cannot talk with certainty about some moral ladder that would allow us to linearly organise each person like contestants and then check whether it is the Christian team or the team of atheists that is winning in the moral race. The apostle Peter in particular would end up somewhere at the very back. If we were to find any differences, we could possibly look within the field of morality in vain. C. S. Lewis adds that this kind of moral competition is not very fair, because it would require our investigation into how the final leaderboard would change if the Christians were not Christians but atheists, and how mixed up the final positions of the atheists would get if they became Christians. In effect, what does it mean to be a Christian and what does it mean to be an atheist? A Christian is somebody who is baptised, or who is baptised and also prays, or who is baptised, prays and goes to church.

We are all in the same boat, attacked by the same temptations, us Christians and us atheists. We ask the same questions and struggle with the same problems. Neither of us are the proclaimers of the final truth, and if we are of goodwill, we want to be its humble servants. Should there be any difference, Christians could be more humble. The greatness of Peter was not in the fact that he did not sin, but rather that after his lapse, he came out and wept bitterly. I am terrified of self-confident people who never made a mistake, visionaries who know the state of things. I am terrified of people whose faith or lack of faith is firmly justified, and they look at us pilgrims with a compassionate smile. The owners of the final truth make me sick be they Christians or atheists. And why not say atheists make me sick, those who cannot even be bothered to follow their argument through and reject faith as such, because their Christian neighbour was not nice to them or because the priest beat them with a cane. It looks like these people were also beaten with a cane by their teacher of logic. I feel sick because of atheists who are too lazy to open a book, but everything is crystal clear to them. Joseph Ratzinger puts this very nicely when he writes that at the bottom of every Christian soul flickers a tiny flame of atheism, and at the bottom of every atheist soul flickers a tiny flame of faith. I like people with the tiny flames very much.

A Christian makes a confession and then carries on sinning

That is not a misconception, but the truth. However, confession does not legalise evil and a very important moment during Holy Confession is regret, a situation where I am not able to look at my past without embarrassment. From regret, comes the desire to put things right: to return what I have stolen, say sorry to the one I shouted at without a reason, and so forth. Thus, the Holy Confession must have this moment of regret, a moment when I long to draw a thick line between me and my past, to put right what is possible and to say sorry for what is no longer possible to put right, to push off from the bottom and try again, but better.

The fact that usually I am not very successful is a different matter and I admit that it looks like people regularly attend Holy Confession without any change or any detectable change. This is somewhat encoded in us humans, and it is necessary to add that the aim of Christianity is not to create a sin-free individual, the aim of Christianity is an individual living in a relationship with God. The church is certainly not an organisation turning out perfect sin-free beings and neither is this its aim.

What one hears from the pulpit as one happens to stumble into a church is the official teaching of the church

Certainly not. The usual misconception is that all priests are of the same opinion and preach what wisdom has been passed on at the seminary. That is not the reality. From time to time, the most wild speculations are heard from the pulpits in direct opposition to the church teaching, very personal perceptions of the world around us, extravagant trips to the realm of natural science, most various glossaries or idiosyncratic political commentaries. With a pinch of humour, the old experienced preachers laid it on the new priests' heart, that when they preach they should not allow for more than three heresys. If any of the atheists want to learn about the official beliefs of the Catholic Church, let him buy Catechism, where all the facts are laid out clearly and concisely. A random visit to an unknown church is like buying a lottery ticket – it might be the winning one.

The Pope forbids the use of condoms in Africa and by that contributes to the spread of AIDS

He actually doesn't. On the contrary, he urges couples to remain faithful, which, let's face it, would stop the AIDS epidemic very effectively, providing his voice was heard. If condoms are to be handed out in Africa, then it should be done by the various governmental and non-governmental organisations and interested activists, and may they continue to do so. This, however, needs time and money. I would be interested to know how many condoms were handed out in Africa for example by those who criticised the Pope during his last visit. And perhaps these critics are not supposed to give advice to the church about what to do and what not to do: if one considers something of great importance one should take care of it by oneself, otherwise it will not get done. It is very easy to sit in an armchair and point out what should be done by whom or should not be done on the other hand. If one thinks condoms should be handed out in Africa, one should get involved.

There is one more important fact that speaks for the Pope: he is the representative of Catholic Christians. Atheists (if there are any in Africa, we should say protestants and members of non-christian religions), in any case, do not have to be restricted by his views, which is true for both Africa and Europe. As far as Catholic Christians are concerned, the important moral codex of Christianity is the Ten Commandments, with its commandment concerning marital faithfulness. On the other hand, compared to the Ten Commandments, to forbid contraception is a statement more within the understanding of encyklika. Should one not obey the very important and binding commandment from the Ten Commandments and have sex outside marriage, there is no reason why one should split hairs when it comes to the lesser binding reality of not using contraception. It is difficult to imagine a Catholic who is breaking the Ten Commandments with ease but pedantically insists on contraception. Using the biblical term, he who has once decided to swallow a camel, does not have to worry about straining a mosquito. Sex outside of marriage with a risky partner breaks two commandments at once, the fifth and the sixth; you are not to kill and not to commit adultery. And what kind of sense would there be to break the Ten Commandments, but insist on tiny details? And would someone really think that the church is so thick to stand against contraception when life is at stake? To bring the discussion to an end, there is no need for the Non-Catholics to feel obliged to the Pope, neither should the Catholics when they feel the urge to break the Ten Commandments.

Perhaps the Pope's truth is aiming deeper here. As an illustration and an example, I would like to present various ecological initiatives. In today's modern green initiatives, Europe started promoting environmentally friendly energy, ecobulbs and hybrid cars. This path is certainly correct and praiseworthy, but does not stand in the way of the basic structure of our civilisation with its belief that an accumulation of things will bring us happiness. Things and experiences we now accumulate with greater care, the current European view and we will still go shopping but now with ecological shopping bags. The church aims at a deeper level inside man, questioning whether it is the circle of things around us that makes us happy. *'For earthly possessions do not satisfy the heart, but going without and being poor in spirit, does.'*[46] says Saint John of the Cross. So, it is not about consuming in the same way or more but with greater care, instead it is about a complete change in our values and lifestyle. The situation concerning AIDS in Africa is similar. Perhaps it is not about engaging in sexual activity the same way, in a different way or different still with better protection, but it is about the feasibility of pursuing true happiness in life by changing partners in different ways through our chaotic promiscuity.

Priests and Christians are trying to convert all atheists to 'Christianity'

God knows that is not true. Christ did not do it this way, although Saint Paul probably did and Christ himself called for it: *Therefore go and make*

---

[46] Jan od Kříže, *Duchovní píseň*. Karmelitánské nakladatelství, Kostelní Vydří, 2000, p. 340

disciples of all nations.[47] Christians believe that God values human freedom highly. On the other hand, what Christians try to do is encourage atheists to follow their argument through to the end. I believe that it is very important for certain questions to be asked: what each of us comes up with is a matter of freedom. Today atheists very often understand the Catholic Church as one of the political organisations, with its own interests and which is trying to gain the highest number of followers from the present market of notions. Christians themselves perhaps do not view it to this extreme. The church is not a political organisation, despite the fact that it is perceived as one by most, and despite the fact that it behaves this way on its own account.

The faith of priests is crystal clear...

It is not. It is strange that atheists (together with Catholics) have a relatively clear picture of what a priest should or should not say, how he should or should not be dressed, where and with whom he should or should not be spending

---

[47] Mat 28,19. (NIV)

his holidays, what he is thinking or not thinking, what he wants or does not want, what kind
of beverages he should or should not consume
in restaurants, what kind of films he should
watch and what kinds he definitely should not,
and they are taken aback when they see that the
real priest and their expectations are two different people. Surprisingly, in this confrontation
both the atheist and the Catholic have a tendency
to correct the priest rather than their expectations. The atheist assumes that the priest is confident and never doubts his faith, he is more or less
a loudspeaker projecting his views and attitudes
that he learnt in the seminary, he is some soulless
product of the seminary directed by the Vatican
or by the bishop's conference, ideologically legible
and firmly placed in his trench. If the priest is not
interested in money and power, working without
expecting anything in return, it is considered
a trick, a strategy of evangelism. A good deed must
be a pretend show used to catch as many sheep
as possible. Paradoxically, the atheist does not
even think that on one hand a priest could *really*
have his own questions and live in tormentous
doubts about his faith. On the other hand and
similarly, it does not occur to him that he would

do a selfless good deed just like that for the sake of good, because he *really* believes in God or he at least believes that to do good is better than to do evil. And by no means could he entertain the thought of both of these joined together in one person – the priest.

... because there is no God

Other times, an atheist cannot even imagine that a priest could really believe in God and he assumes that similarly to him, a priest must be an atheist and therefore make a business out of his faith by brainwashing his sheep. There is no God, everybody knows that, is the atheist belief. Then a question comes to mind, as to why priests, in effect, do what they do. Either it is because priesthood offers a good and comfortable lifestyle, or eventually it could be the wildest orgies taking place behind the monastery walls, as money is being accumulated and varied sexual practices take place. It is a paradox that these kind of fantasies say more about what is going on inside the atheist mind, rather than about what takes place behind the monastery walls. A meeting with an educated member of a holy order who is obviously very happy in his monastic poverty, stands far from atheist fantasies and a hypothesis has to be thought up to justify the existence of such a man. Perhaps he was deceived himself, maybe he is good at putting on a front, maybe he has got millions hidden in the Vatican somewhere under a pillow, who knows? A relatively simple explanation that this is all due to the fact that he really believes hardly crosses the atheist mind. Providing this could happen, many other unsettling questions would follow.

The definition of Christianity, as well as what Christians strive for and what their God is like is general knowledge

Atheists know nothing about this, but generally they think they do. Especially in this country a remarkable gap has been formed between what atheists imagine when they hear the terms 'Christians', 'God', 'church' and so forth, and what Christians themselves imagine when they hear these terms. The usual perception is to describe some perception of God (the punishing triangle with an eye, and old man on a cloud, a great horologist or anything else) and then successfully fight this image. Yes, it is easy to fight *this kind* of God, but at the end of the debate, to their surprise, both atheist and believer agree that this God does not exist. In the Czech media, Christians are presented as a movement striving for property restitution, cathedral ownership, prohibition of sex before marriage, together with contraception and abortions, so something like a moralising spruce-up society. The reality is different. First, Christians are interested in, let's say it in a clumsy way, the relationship with the numinous: eternity, existential leaning of man to the absolute, consumption by faith, the step into the darkness or the abyss of faith, the relationship with holiness, the lifelong attempt to respond to a task, in order for man to become the image of God. Second, a certain attempt to find an answer to existential questions: why I exist, where I come from and where I am going, and so on. Only now, third, comes the collection of moral ideas, and fourth a certain worldview, explanation of the world, conviction that thanks to the existence of providence the world makes sense.[48]

---

[48] Paraphrasing Bochenski, J., *Mezi logikou a vírou.* Barrister & Principal, 2001, Brno.

In different debates with atheists, unmistakably the first subject discussed is always sex, and the second subject is money and restitution. This phenomenon is remarkable in itself and undoubtedly points to what the minds of fellow citizens are predominantly preoccupied with.

The Catholic Church is a united monolithic organisation with one faith, one view and one aim

It is not. There are many different currents here, movements and internal conflicts, different spiritualities, orthodox and liberal wings, intellectual and charismatic, it is more like a rippling sea reaching to many sides rather than a united river or closed marching squad. This state of things could make most Christians feel sorry, but it has one great advantage! The Catholic Church is not a sect with only one opinion. Catholic Christians are members of most of the political parties here and abroad. Then if an atheist meets the political or religious views of a Christian, in no time he could meet another Christian whose views are exactly the opposite. The atheist is even more confused when he realises that both of these Catholic believers consider themselves orthodox. It kind of reminds me of the Jewish anecdote where *Rabbi X says x, Rabbi Y says y and you say that they are both right, despite the fact that x and y are impossible to put together! – You are also right though...* An outsider would expect that at least in fundamental matters, unity prevails, for example, when referring to the existence of God or of the human soul. That is possibly true, but I suggest that the atheist carries out a small survey directed towards individual believers, with a question asking what they imagine lies behind the word 'God' and 'soul' and I am convinced that he will be very surprised. On another occasion, the atheist is genuinely surprised when he finds out that a priest's opinion stands in direct opposition to that of another priest or even of the bishop.

To become a Christian one must absolutely be connected to the restitution of wealth and return of the cathedral to the church

... eventually even vote for the Christian-democrats in the election. This is one of the most widespread and serious misconceptions, to understand the church as a political party. Atheists often refuse faith in God exactly because of the cathedral or restitution. Faith in God is one thing, attending church is another and (political) activity of the church is a third. I believe that what we lack here to a great extent is this exactly: both atheists and Christians are under the impression that to attend church means to join some political wing, participate in a given political programme and have a specific view of the restitution and the cathedral. But that is not the case. Different Catholics are members of different political parties and hold different views on different political concepts. Perhaps the time will come, when there will be no Saint Vitus Cathedral, neither wealth nor political choice. But still the joined prayer of the Holy Mass will remain in churches or flats, purely because it is needed. Perhaps the time will come, when different prosperous holy orders of today will cease to exist. Perhaps the time will come, when there is no wealth and the cathedral will be torn down, with no churches or priories. Then still prayer will remain and the partaking in the Holy Mass, not as an agreement with a given political project, but only as the Holy Mass, within the church itself, which will not be perceived as state made or made by any other institution, but only as a society as an organism without any connection to any other political party, without any ambitions to claim back property, without any ambitions to influence the latest election.

I believe that this unspoken vision closes the gates of church for many atheists, that when I accept faith in God (or just begin to consider it), it would also mean a certain political commitment, an agreement with the assumed stance of the 'Vatican', for example concerning the condoms in Africa which is unacceptable and laughed at by those around me. It is necessary to repeat it again: God is not orange or blue.

Religion is an opium for mankind

I do not know who quoted the opposite but they stated that opium became the religion of mankind. It is true. If at least atheism was the alternative! From Marx's sentence about the opium of mankind, it appears as if people knew the intentions of history, how to live a meaningful life and only the religions are somewhat spoiling it for us. They are an opium of mankind leading us all astray. But do completely and truly happy atheists really exist somewhere, satisfied atheists who discovered and found the true meaning of things? Excuse me for asking, but I would be interested to know. And you, current scientists, architects, sculptors and artists, modern sexologists and psychologists, singers and actresses, moderators and entertainers, famous sportsmen, philosophers, modern and postmodern, have you found anything? Is it about marriage and children, as the last century thought, or about childless *singles*, this century's view? In love for one life, or for one night, in power, in fame, money, sport or philosophy?

Isn't the entire current world of the rich western Europe nothing more than an annotation under the line in the book of Ecclesiastes? Doesn't the everyday reality remind us that no new crossroads or soap operas, neither golf nor new culinary recipes, or sex with a new partner in a different way, or new countries with new friends, or shopping in new shops, or new football matches, or new films, or regular exercise will bring a relief from the tormentous voice within our soul for no more than a few minutes? We made Europe a waiting room for death. We try to furnish it to the best of our ability but it is still only a waiting room. Is the life of rich modern western Europe with all its ideas nothing but proof that atheism used up all its bullets, but did not manage to offer any alternative? We can jump with a parachute from the universal base ISS, eat beef steaks from cows who were regularly massaged and drink wine with golden leaves, we can do anything, but the tormentous voice in our soul is not silenced. What else have you got to offer? What else can you do? What else should be pulled out of the hat? In general, is it not obvious during the New Year celebrations that Europe is dancing its *ghost dance* on the ruins of values? And I would like to ask, is happiness our life's ultimate goal? I think that one of the few interesting attempts in Europe are the trappists and some other contemplative monasteries.

Jonas, Ecclesiastes and Job stood by my cradle and became my godparents and the guides of modern civilisation. Ecclesiastes guides me with his ironic smile through the Earth with an unlimited credit card, with Job I step down to the underground of the soul and with Jonas I am trying to run away in vain. Before atheists criticise Christianity they should take into account themselves, where they are at, and if they have any ideas, they could share them. And if there really is no God, how come that we are here, and how come we are asking all these questions? Why are we banging on the gates of heaven with our questions?

The Catholic Church keeps people ignorant and stands against free scientific research. Faith is not compatible with science

Thank God that today there are numerous texts dealing with the theme of science and faith and they offer a different picture to the communist primary schools. It is worth listing as a reminder: during the second half of the 12th century, the first European universities with undergraduate and postgraduate studies came into being, emphasising reason and stressing the importance of looking for arguments in favour of both conflicting parties.[49] Why were these kinds of universities not created in Ancient Greece, Africa, Asia or anywhere else? Why only in Europe? In the 13th century, Franciscan monk Robert Bacon laid

---

[49] Woods, Jr, T. E., *Jak katolická církev budovala západní civilizaci.* Res claritas, Praha, 2008, p. 42–56.

the foundations of modern scientific methodology, Saint Albert the Great (about 1200–1280) laid the foundations of natural science in the field of today's physics, biology, psychology etc. and became the patron of natural scientists. Thirty-five craters on the Moon are named after Jesuit natural scientists and mathematicians, and why is that? Pater Clavius was the chairman of the committee that created the Gregorian calendar in 1582, introduced by Pope Gregory XIII. Jesuit P. Francesco Grimaldi discovered diffraction of light. Monk Gregor Mendel laid the foundation of genetics in 1865. Belgian priest Georges Lemaître was the first to propose the theory of the universe later known as the 'Big Bang' in 1927.

If the Catholic Church denied free thinking, good and beauty, and was an obscurus organisation to this extent as it is presented, how come so many cathedrals were established at its centre? Worship could be held simply in barns or purpose built buildings resembling the communistic panel block. The building trade of the Middle Ages would undoubtedly manage this better and with much less expenditure than the York Cathedral or the one in Vyssi Brod or the Golden Crown Cathedral. From the heart of the church the jewels of cathedrals and the gregorian choral gush out, Fra Angelico and Thomas Aquinas. I consider it symptomatic to compare art of the 'dark' Middle Ages, with what communism has shown us: concrete blocks, soulless music, mass art, literature of socialistic realism. The period's fundamental mindset, which people's heads are filled with, is always somehow reflected in architecture, art, music, statues, pictures, philosophy, literature, science and the relationship with the surrounding environment.

It is not despite the church, but thanks to the church, that brains are being born at its centre which decorate the Sistine Chapel and built Saint Vitus Cathedral – or the most beautiful baroque church in Lechovice on the spot, that must have been chosen with a spark of ingenuity.

In this church, priest Prokop Diviš had his First Mass – the discoverer of the lightning rod. Today communism ceased to exist, but I am not entirely sure, percentage wise, how much of the modern art of today could stand to be compared to the paintings, statues and architecture of these 'dark' Middle Ages. On top of that, it is worth calculating how many people lived in Europe at that time in total and how many today, and what educational and self-development opportunities were available at that time and what is available today, what was technically possible in architecture with the materials available, and what is available today. The end result of today's efforts appear very pitiful to me, despite our education system and so many endless possibilities that have been proclaimed. Is the Catholic Church really such a great enemy of beauty, good and truth?

A QUESTION MARK
WRITTEN IN THE AIR

Many years ago, my friend and I went hiking in the Adrspach Rocks. It was about minus twelve degrees with fresh snow and we slept without a tent at the top of the sandstone lumps and drank whisky until we ran out, and that happened quite quickly. We smoked short pipes and we felt great.

On our way back we had the nice feeling of those who managed an endeavour in the terrain and whose expedition turned out to be a success and who, like Jacob a long time ago, fought the absolute and came out fairly well. For time spent in the terrain always becomes spiritual experience and often spiritual battle, and a man grows up faster in the mountains.

On route we planned to stop off in a pleasantly heated building, where at the time, young Christians had a spiritual retreat and where I was supposed to say something about Darwin, evolution, Christianity and nature. We shook the snow off our backpacks, followed by the smokey smell of mountain pine trees and tobacco as we entered the hall, and the young people, boys and girls aged fourteen to thirty-five, were friendly and likeable.

They suggested we pray before the lecture, which I was pleased to agree to, because I am a conservative Catholic. Let's pray through a song! And then it hit me. The song was chosen in connection to the theme of the lecture, and it was a well-known interactive song called 'Who Is the Creator?' and not only the cheerful sixth formers, but also the thirty to thirty-five-year-old men were showing the rippling sea, the twinkling stars, and even the prickly hedgehogs faithfully and with enthusiasm, and I was quietly asking myself whether some of us here had managed to grow up yet or not, and I was thinking about how feminine the current Catholic Church is, with all its cantates, hosannas and guitar ditties that only meet the needs of sixteen-year-old romantic girls and that is it. And I was thinking about Ken Kesey and his *One Flew over the Cuckoo's Nest* and it came to me that perhaps the current Catholic Church is like the great institution, where under the direction of senior sisters with their sister hats, skirts and baroque laces, we all volunteer to stay inside, because we are too afraid to leave. The male Catholics in the Middle Ages had it good, they had their knighthoods, but what about us? And when I am asked by journalists what my thoughts are about the current Catholic Church, I never have anything to say, but when I close my eyes, I see the thirty-year-old men, drawing a question mark in the air, and then pointing their fingers to heaven, shouting *'our Father God'*.

MEETING WITH YOUTH

To begin with, I receive the routine email,
Dear Father, we would like to organise a youth
meeting in our dioceses ... we are inviting different experts ... we would be grateful if ... I write
back that I am no expert, I do not understand
youth, I am a bit dry, my speeches are not interesting and surely better and more willing speakers can be found, and unfortunately my diary
is already quite full, so with regret... The writer
is stubborn and contacts me again and again
through email, and then on the phone, and so
I resign and try to come up with business to be
taken care of on this long journey to make it

count, and at this, I arrive on the given day at the given place.

There are young people all around me, with smiles and orange tags around their necks. At the reception, I explain with slight embarrassment why I am here. The girl looks at me as if she has known me for a long time, gives me my pre-printed name tag, and says that she will shortly send for an animator to accompany me. I am not quite sure who the 'animator' is; to entertain myself I am trying to imagine what sort of creature he could be, perhaps a cross between a crocodile and a caiman? The girl willingly explains that it is the person who brings fellowship to life – in the gathering they must still find another animator and together they will make the whole meeting come alive. Oh!.. So this is how it works.

A young likeable boy turns up and really intro-duces himself as the 'animator' and says that he will accompany me, showing me to the next table right away. They are very well organised. The girl sitting there asks whether I want to be reimbursed for my travel costs. I tell her that I had enough of my own responsibilities to attend to, and therefore will gladly leave the financial worries to the organisers. The girl is consulting another likeable girl, soon coming to the conclusion that they will gladly cover my expenses.

"That is very kind of you," I reply.

"It is enough if you give us a copy of your MOT certificate," the likeable girl says.

"I have not got a copy of it with me," I answered. Should I have brought it? I asked myself. I have not really read the emails, who knows what was said.

"That does not matter," says the likeable girl, "give me the original MOT and we will make a copy of it."

But I have not got that with me either. It is not even supposed to be kept in the car, is it?

The likeable girls discuss this amongst themselves for a while.

"Never mind," she lets out with a smile.

"Never mind," I let out with a smile. I am thinking to myself that I am amongst my own.

The animator leads me to the main hall, full of young people.

"Here is where all the speakers will present," he explains. "You will walk onto the platform, introduce yourself and explain to the youth why they should attend *your* lecture in particular."

"But I do not want anybody to attend my lecture!" I object. "I am not assertive and I do not want to convince anybody of anything, especially not to make them listen to my thoughts!" I am already somewhat unnerved. They invite me, yet they want me to find my own audience!

"You have to do this," the animator explains, "all the speakers have to do this," he insists. If only, if only. But the animator is young, he was born after '89 and he does not know my generation. We were very used to saying no and well taught to say it, and we knew very well that we were not obliged to do anything, despite the consequences. Today some see this as pigheaded stubbornness. We call it strong will that helped us survive.

"Well, then I have some bad news for you," I say to the animator. "We are staying down here. Deal with it as you please. I am a shy boy," I explain.

The animator suspects that we both have a problem, and I feel sorry for him, and I can tell from his face what he is thinking. Why was he the one to be landed with such a fool?

"At least say your name and the name of your lecture," he pleads.

"Okay," I agree.

Another likeable girl backstage is asking us to cut it short, we are running late already. I happily agree to that. The speakers before me introduce themselves and as instructed, they try to persuade the youth to go to *their* lecture in particular. I say my name and the name of the lecture and hand over the microphone as agreed. I was the only one who was scrupulous.

The animator takes me to the room where I will be speaking and on my way, I unexpectedly run into my friend Joey. We greet each other cheerfully, we met right in front of the coffee machine, we take it as a sign and we both go for hot chocolate, the animator refuses to join, thanking us for the offer. "What are you going to see?" I ask. "The Joy of Being a Woman," replies Joey. "I am the only guy going, the rest are just girls." "That is very surprising," I reply.

The little meeting room where I am speaking is full. Wow! It was possible even without assertiveness. I speak for an hour and a half, as agreed, several intelligent questions asked. Then an older man asks whether I have brought any of my books along with me. I have not brought any books. "I never bring my books with me," I explain. "That is a pity," says the man. If only, if only. If people want to come to my lecture, that is their decision, and if during the conversation sparks begin to fly and the atmosphere is pleasant, I am very glad. I like it when during the 'flight' the audience does not even move and listens as everyone comes to a consensus. And then I find it embarrassing when the fine threads of a new relationship are cut with the last sentence, an invitation to pick up my signed book from the table at the back, available at a discount, for those who are interested – that is too much for me, I really am a shy boy. The only time I am not shy is when the wind of the lecture whisks me up and we fly together, but before or after – no chance.

From the animator, I was given a beautiful candle for my lecture and even the New Testament on CD, so that I can listen to it nicely in my car, he explains. "Now, all I need to do is buy a CD player for my car," I try to say thank you clumsily. Immediately after my performance, independently of each other, two members of the audience stop me, they liked my speech, and would really like for me to repeat it in their home parishes near the border. We exchange details and discuss further correspondence.

On my way, I am thinking about the fact that in this whole wide world only two kinds of real trouble exist. The first is when your lecture is a failure. The second is when it is a success.

After the lecture, a joined Holy Mass takes place, my animator takes me to the vestry, where there are bishops and priests in charge of the youth pastoral care, as well as many other priests acquainted and unacquainted.

The music playing is from Hosanna, the band is above average with melancholy piano like from the band *Mission*, the pianist on the keyboard does exactly as he pleases, touching on jazz in places. He is very good. To begin with, there is an interactive song, the priest up front is showing everyone the right moves and the youth repeat them, their thumbs and pinkies stretched by their ears, pretending they are on the phone to God, and with their hands over their hearts, symbolising our love for each other. All the priests around me are participating – and I would also gladly join in, but I cannot, I really cannot because I do not have the right joy, and so I refrain from a spring in my step. Excited Catholics and smiles all around. Boys and girls exchanging looks, sparks flying in every direction and connecting people in the hall. One almost hears the hiss of electricity and the flicker in their eyes is like from Saint Elias' fire. "We met at a Holy Mass," I heard many times from dreamy long haired girls. Surely, it must have somehow been planned by God.

A girl and a boy give the bishop a bouquet of flowers thanking him for finding the time to come to be among us. There would be logic to it, if the youth themselves somehow spontaneously decided to meet somewhere and the bishop got up and went to see them. However, I have a vague feeling that the whole event was organised by the bishop's office.

Exchanging the peace greeting, we all hold hands like during the Holy Mass for children, and then we shake them, because we share the same spirit. The Holy Mass for youth is a Holy Mass for youth and a man should know what he is letting himself into, or not go at all. Do the youth share the same feelings as I or do the moves really correspond with their inner being? What if we all think that this is what the youth like, and the youth think that this is what the older generations like, and out of love, nobody wants to spoil it for the others?

After the Holy Mass, I say goodbye to my helpful animator, thank him for his patience (it was

not easy for him either, poor chap), symboli-
cally I meet Joey at the coffee machine, and the
animator refuses to join, thanking us for the
offer. "What have you found out?", I ask over
today's second hot chocolate. "I should give birth
to as many kids as possible, no matter what,
because a gift ought to be accepted," proclaims
Joseph with a mysterious smile. We are drinking
our hot chocolate as we say goodbye. Joseph is
leaving for a study year and we will not see each
other. He comes with me all the way to the car.

Thank goodness I ran into Joseph.

LIFE AS AN ORIENTATION RACE

I.

Seeking God's will: the ever-present topic debated by penitents and Catholic students. At which university does God want me to study? Does God want me to join the seminary, or get married? Or should it be a Holy Order? And if marriage, who is the wife God has chosen for me? Where does she live – and will I be able to recognise her when we meet for the first time? Or more subtle: Is it God's wish for me to spend a year abroad during my studies? And if so, where exactly am I to go? In the same way as Jeremiah was called to be a prophet in his mother's womb,

"Before I formed you in the womb I knew you, before you were born I set you apart; I appointed you as a prophet to the nations."[50]

Before Jeremiah is able to do good or evil, before he is able to earn his calling, the same could perhaps be true about our situation. Similarly to Jeremiah or John the Baptist, we are also called to our task on this Earth long before our birth. From conversations with many students, I get the feeling from time to time that they perceive their life as an orientation race that has been set and planned in advance by God. Then the task of the Christian is to seek God's will and in the same way as a runner looks for the correct path with his compass, so is the Christian to always seek God's will in prayer about his future wife, future school, the program for today's afternoon or the sentence that he is about to say. It has already been written somewhere and now I have to aim as close as possible to the life trajectory which has been drawn for me since the beginning of time. The task of the day is to follow, as closely as possible, the line of God's will.

---

[50] Jer 1,5. (NIV)

Sometimes it is us priests who promote this kind of understanding of our relationship with God through our sermons, which our acolytes rightly and with a bit of irony renamed as a 'Milky Way' homily. It is about the wedding ceremony, in which the priest states that before the Almighty God created the heavens and the earth, before he created this strange universe, before he created the stars and the Milky Way, before our planet came into being from a hot dust, he had chosen you, John, and you, Mary, so that you could stand here at the altar today to promise your love, respect and faithfulness... and John and Mary look at each other happily – yes, our marriage is something of fate, stellar, before our time, predestined only for the two of us, from our birth we were growing up for each other – without even knowing it! – then we met for the first time and understood, and sparks came flying and now we are only affirming what God has planned and wanted for us a long time ago. Our relationship is not a biological coincidence, but something sacred that has been written for the two of us in heaven since the beginning of the ages. Before God created me in my mother's womb, he had given us to each other. And the acolytes who have known John and Mary for many years, and have also been aware of their many previous relationships and escapades, are smiling nicely at them.

II.

I mean, in the end, why not? But if I understood my life as an orientation race taking a route prepared in advance, if I perceived my life as something that had been set since before the ages, telling me exactly what I should be doing today in the afternoon between two and three o'clock and every other minute of my life, I am slightly afraid creativity would no longer be a part of it. Then I would, in effect, become only a robot that, with the help of the prayer sensors, tries to be guided to the right path with no other purpose. I am not sure, I do not want to make fun of it too much, but I think that the reality is more complex, that my own spiritual creativity is asked of me, that God takes me much more seriously than a mere spiritual orientation runner, that apart from my obedience, my own ideas are also required of me. We are not pre-programmed machines, buzzing through some life journey, we are free in the full meaning of the word. We are created beings, who should also create.

Rabbi Jonathan Sacks offers an exciting lecture on the story of Noah and Abraham.[51] Noah is given the highest mark by the Holy Scribes, *"Noah was a righteous man, blameless among the people of his time, and he walked with God."*[52] Only a few in the Old Testament were given this high a rank. And still, at the end of Noah's life, the awkward scene takes place in which Noah gets drunk and his two sons Shem and Japheth cover him walking backwards, with their faces turned away, so as not to see their father's nakedness. How could this have happened? Rabbi Sacks explains that Noah always and in everything followed God's will, fulfilling all God's commands precisely: he made the ark exactly according to God's commands with all the floors and windows, measurements and details, which the Bible offers plentifully. *"Noah did everything just as God commanded him."*[53] Then the story goes on, Noah is commanded to take the animals into the ark, *"And Noah did all that the Lord commanded*

---

[51] Sacks, J., *Covenant and Conversation. Genesis: The Book of the Beginnings.* Maggid Book and the Orthodox Union. New Milford, USA, 2009, p. 43-47.

[52] Gn 6,9. (NIV)

[53] Gn 6,22. (NIV)

him."[54] This sentence is then repeated once more *"Pairs of clean and unclean animals, of birds and of all creatures that move along the ground, male and female, came to Noah and entered the ark, as God had commanded Noah."*[55]

Several fast paced sentences follow, in which the hundred and fifty day disastrous flood is described. Then the storytelling comes to an abrupt halt and slows down to reach an unbearable point. Noah is waiting for forty days and then lets out a raven that flies around unable to find a place to sit, then he lets out a dove that comes back, then after seven days another dove, then another dove, which then comes back with an olive branch, and then another dove, which does not return. Then Noah waits and waits, and nobody knows why, until he receives a command from the Lord to leave the ark, and only then does he come out. Noah always follows God's commands exactly.

The question is, though, what did Noah say when he found out about God's plan to destroy the whole Earth? What did he say when he found out that God wanted to save Noah and his family,

---

[54] Gn 7,5. (NIV)
[55] Gn 7,8–9. (NIV)

but destroy the rest of humanity? What did he say when he found out that God wanted to destroy even the animals? What did he say? The answer is – nothing.[56] Noah does not say a single word in the Bible. Noah always and in everything obeys the will of God diligently – but meanwhile the world is destroyed! After the flood, Noah only keeps on waiting. Midrash[57] says, if the world is in pieces, it is not necessary to wait in the ark for God's command to come out, to renew the Earth, surely we do not require God's special permission! And if a man does not care about other people, it is no surprise that in the end he does not end up well himself, hence the story of Noah's nakedness.

Later, Abraham ends up in a similar situation. He is also told that a lot of people are to be destroyed, the whole town of Sodom. Noah and Abraham know that a catastrophe is upon them, but each of them act completely differently. Abraham knows very well that Sodom is a town of sin, and great sin, but despite the fact that he is not

---

[56] Sacks, J., *Covenant and Conversation. Genesis: The Book of the Beginnings.* Maggid Book and the Orthodox Union. New Milford, USA, 2009, p. 43-47.

[57] Midrash is a term used in reference to the early rabinistic interpretations of Torah.

asked to, he is trying the impossible, and in one of the most impressive dialogues between a man and God that has ever been recorded, he tries to negotiate to the best of his ability. Furthermore, the people of Sodom are not Abraham's relatives, they are complete strangers to him! When his son Lot is taken captive during the small local battle, Abraham sets off immediately to rescue him, and he manages to free Lot. Abraham could have failed in his effort, but Noah had never even tried.[58]

III.

I think the answer is clear in the comparison between Noah and Abraham. Abraham is surely listening to God's will and fulfills it he sets off from his town into the unknown and follows God's commands. However, apart from that, he is not shy to come to Yahweh, present his arguments and fight when he thinks that he ought to. On one hand, Abraham follows God's will until it is unbearable – it is said that if we do not

---

[58] Sacks, J., *Covenant and Conversation. Genesis: The Book of the Beginnings.* Maggid Book and the Orthodox Union. New Milford, USA, 2009, p. 43-47.

occasionally get shivers down our spine whilst reading the Old Testament, then we must not be reading it carefully enough – as he goes to sacrifice his beloved son Isaac on the other hand, Abraham is certainly not just a passive individual following God's will. Obedience is a useful thing, but it is not the whole story!

In addition, not even in Abraham's life does God speak every day, and the Scripture documents long years and even decades when God is quiet and nothing of great importance is taking place.

I believe that God will bless all the students, no matter which school or foreign exchange they decide on, and when it comes to marriage, I believe that God will bless every relationship and every decision of two free people, that He accepts this decision as it is, and that He respects our choice. I believe that as God blesses the righteous Noah and the righteous Abraham, He also blesses us. Apart from that, I believe that God will bless all marriages of all of His people who decided to get married according to God's will or not (who knows), I believe that if not God's blessing, then God's love accompanies me in my sin, and that God will not let go of me, no matter what I do. I believe that God's love somehow even follows us, those who sometimes wander without a map or a compass, lost somewhere in the woods, not knowing which way to go. I believe that God does not want me to obey His commands only, but also to act and fight, speak and strive. It is Abraham who will become the symbol of faith for the world, not Noah, and perhaps this is not a coincidence.

THE CHURCH OF SINNERS

Once I gave a lecture at the Faculty of Natural Sciences as part of a philosophy and biology series and everyone who attended got into a massive argument, lecturers and students alike, all against one another, with an atmosphere of great unrest. When the lecture came to an end, we all went to the canteen to wash it down with juice, coffee or even something stronger, and nobody took it personally. I remember how we held each other around our shoulders and all that had happened was understood as an intellectual exercise, which moved us forward, and if my opponent was possibly wrong, his mistake still forced me to think and justify why I thought he was wrong, and whether he could possibly have a point? This is more or less the case in science – it is better to live in constant, neverending doubt, than to be firmly rooted in one's misconception. The truth is that when it comes to science, the problem is not so much what we do not know, but rather what we think we know for certain – which could be a fatal error. One of the differences between science and religion is the fact that science knows no dogmas and the daily bread of scientists is to live in the insecurity of doubts about how the world is really organised.

I realised how much I miss this in the Catholic environment. What we are good at is distinguishing 'us' from 'them', to 'us', who know how things work, and so we pray, sincerely striving to achieve something, firmly set in the circle of our trench, and the rest are 'them', the modernists and liberals (who we feel are not as pious as us) or candle grannies who spend hours sitting in churches (who we feel are more pious than us). The common denominator of these or other groups is their spontaneous lustration, in which they decide who is friend and who is foe, who has the right faith and who does not.

While the official Catholic Church has canonised some believers as saints and never pronounced anybody as condemned, here it is the other way round: who gets to go to heaven is not clear, but who is going to hell is indisputable. The rest who are not trinitarian or trinitarian to an extreme, who mistakenly chose the Vatican Neo-Catholicism instead of the Trident truth, who put certain orders higher than others, together with parishes or the Catholic Church itself, or fatally underestimated the contribution of these orders and movements, to their own detriment, believing that everyone who is of a different opinion to themselves cannot be an honest Christian, and is on a straight pass in the direction of damnation.

It is only in Antarctica or the nameless hills of the deserted Andes that we fully grasp how provincial, domesticated and peddling our picture of God is, thought up somewhere on this tiny planet in a remote village of the majestic universe and all the fights and accusations are suddenly comical, insular or how to put it. From the universal point of view, a man begins to respect different ways of honouring God from praying in tongues, to different trinitarian worship. From the bivouac on the high plateau the difference between the

Vatican and trident liturgy is wiped away and the only thing that counts is the state of one's heart. It is possible to honour God, but not to understand him. Only children need heroes good and bad, the mature adult is aware that even heroes have their faults and cowards their virtues.

Do we really grasp, precisely, who God is, what his exact wishes are here on Earth, and how we are to practice our faith in detail? What has to happen to make us understand that we all pray to the same God, that we all long for good, that almost nobody among us is entirely evil, but we simply all perceive certain things differently? Vladimir Solovjov introduces, in his bitter Tale of the Anti-Christ, the idea of the complete and ecumenical reconciliation of all Christians – however, this only takes place after great persecution, reducing the numbers of Christians down to the last three: Orthodox, Catholic and Protestant. Only then are they united by a common fate. Sometimes I ask myself, how many of us Catholics would have to remain, in order to make us understand that a different way of living in faith is neither a personal insult nor an insult to God or the Catholic church. I have great longing for a church in which at the end of our disputes we leave together for the canteen to wash it all down with juice or something stronger. I long for a church of seekers, a church of the humble, who do not think that the one who sees things differently is pegged as the heretic in the first round. We are very good at spotting the splinters in other people's eyes. Anthony de Mello has made a very sharp observation concerning believers as crueler than other people, because they tend to sacrifice others too easily for the sake of their truth.

I completely understand that sometimes the church has to turn to the last possible solution, excommunication, but at least in the past few decades, every time this happened, it was after very careful and very painful consideration, with a constant striving for reconciliation. If I live with God, and I am right, then life is very difficult with me. For those around me who are wrong, surely must not live with God, otherwise they would be able to see things the way I do. Since the way I see things is the way that God sees things, it is worth me proclaiming the Truth, be it convenient or not, no matter what, in the name of the Father and the Son and the Holy Spirit. However, I am surrounded by like-minded people, who posses a slightly different Truth to me, but also live with

God. What happens when they start using their Truth against me, whether it is appropriate or not, in the name of the Father and the Son and the Holy Spirit? Then we are only one step away from catastrophe.

Only Christ could claim about himself that he is the Truth. The rest of us are not of it or in possession of it, but should only be the humble servants of it. The point is not whether we are right but whether we are in the Truth, as Radl nicely puts it. I am not the owner of Christ, I want to be his humble servant. Only Jesus Christ is the Truth, not I! There is only one universal and unchanging Truth, but it is in heaven, here down on Earth we have only tiny shards, fragments of truth, if not for any other reason, then because our understanding is limited.

This is where, the damned by many, postmodern relativity came from – it was at the time when philosophers realised that it was none other than the owners of the final truth who built Auschwitz and gulags in Kolyma. It is a great temptation of all the fundamentalists to establish heaven on Earth, to separate the wheat from the chaff and make the bad disappear from the face of the Earth. A fundamentalist is someone who wants to pass on their vision to the entire world, the easy way or the hard way.

In the same way as recommended and forbidden books used to exist, it is my impression that from time to time we think about the priests and the non-qualified, considering some of them as 'good', of us, and then there are the others. I want to say something futile – the reality is more complex. The man with a different Truth to me may not be evil possessed after all, perhaps not even by the evil of modernism or paid by the Freemasons. Perhaps he is quite an ordinary Christian, prone to mistakes just like me, and maybe at night we pray the same Rosary, we both share in Sacraments, because we think that it is important, and we both only see things through a different lens. It is easy to see enemies of Truth, Church and God in those who are of a different opinion to us. *It is very difficult to see in different-minded people, the friends of truth, church and God* because this kind of view undermines my stability to a great extent and makes my position as the owner of the last, the only and the final truth, relative.

EPILOGUE

Reflecting on the Moravian pop-up nativity after a festive glass of mulled wine

When the well-wishers had left, it was not possible to move in the Bethlehem cave. All the gifts were properly lined up and put away under the supervision of Saint Joseph. Shoes given by the shoemaker, a child-sized embroidered waistcoat from the tailor, a loaf of bread from the baker, ice skates from a nameless schoolboy, a tray of cakes and a pot of milk from a peasant woman and several kegs of unknown content brought in on a sledge by the carolers, took up most of the space. In front of the cave on the flattened grass, following the many choirs that came to sing to Baby Jesus, a merry lamb brought from an unknown flock was grazing and sniffing the scrunched up newspapers left behind. Jacob and Vavra along with their double bass had finished playing and were on their way home just as the poor were. The Valachs, instructed by the angel to make the long journey to Bethlehem, finished singing their 'haidom haidom tydlidom' and followed their foreman, who still got up after a full day's work and joined the others in coming. Only the angel with the star and the banner which read *Gloria in Excelsis Deo* was flying about over the cave, left and right, so that the banner would remain nice and flat in the wind and the text would be well displayed. Those interested in rocking Baby Jesus came out empty handed due to the sturdiness of Jesus' manger. Instead they sang along to Mary's lullaby, quietly humming 'sleep, baby, sleep'. Right next to the manger, there stood a small milk jug from the shepherds and two sheep skins to cover the newborn's feet, for the men had heard the infant was naked and had nothing. In between the donkey and the ox, there were apples and pears, baked treats together with silver coins handed out by Mary to the singers on behalf of Baby Jesus. A pot of sheep cheese stood in the corner, as well as a couple of eggs from Andrew and Matthew, and milk and honey for porridge donated from an unspecified Moravian region. Some of the presents were given selflessly, others were offered with the hope of God's blessing in return.

However, it all needed to be left behind. Nobody apart from Mary and Joseph knew that God sometimes plays hide-and-seek with people and only ever reveals His very next step. Joseph had already experienced this: once after weeks of anxious deliberation, he decided to secretly let Mary go and only at the very last minute, when he was ready to do it, he had one of his first dreams. In the very last moment possible, God speaks. That is why, instructed by another dream, Joseph got up immediately during the night, took Mary along with Baby Jesus and fled to Egypt, taking only the bare essentials that the donkey could carry. Gold, incense and myrrh stayed behind in the cave, together with the rest of the gifts. Mary still managed to open the door to the cage at the very last minute, in which five coins were counted by the little quail as the cuckoo sang sweetly, and the Holy Family headed south under the veil of darkness while the earth was breathing in its sleep, and somewhere in the distance one could just about hear the merry choir on their way home, playing the bagpipes and singing together.

So, it came to pass that in the morning the soldiers who appeared with swords and spears only found the selection of gifts lined up by the lonely ox with almond eyes that was quietly chewing hay from the trough. If Joseph had worried about the presents, or if out of tiredness he had decided to wait until dawn, the history of salvation would have been played out considerably different to what the carolers had in mind.

ABOUT THE AUTHOR

—————————————

Marek Vácha is a Catholic priest and head of the Department of Ethics and Humanities of the 3rd Faculty of Medicine at Charles University, Prague. Born in Brno in 1966, he studied molecular biology, genetics and theology. He has been a member of two expeditions to Antarctica and lived in the Sept-Fons trappist monastery in France. Vácha is the parish priest of the Lechovice Parish and chaplain to the Roman Catholic Academic Parish at the Church of the Most Holy Salvador.